The Politics of Faculty Unionization

The Experience of Three New England Universities

Gordon B. Arnold

BERGIN & GARVEY
Westport, Connecticut • London

Library of Congress Cataloging-in-Publication Data

Arnold, Gordon B., 1954–
    The politics of faculty unionization : the experience of three New England universities / Gordon B. Arnold.
        p. cm.
    Includes bibliographical references and index.
    ISBN 0–89789–716–1 (alk. paper)
    1. College teachers' unions—New England—Case studies. 2. Collective bargaining—College teachers—New England—Case studies. 3. Universities and colleges—New England—Administration—Case studies. 4. University of Connecticut. 5. University of Rhode Island. 6. University of Massachusetts (System). I. Title.
    LB2335.865.U6 A75   2000
    331.88'1137874—dc21   00–037814

British Library Cataloguing in Publication Data is available.

Library of Congress Catalog Card Number: 00–037814
ISBN: 0–89789–716–1

First published in 2000

Bergin & Garvey, 88 Post Road West, Westport, CT 06881
An imprint of Greenwood Publishing Group, Inc.
www.greenwood.com

Printed in the United States of America

∞™

The paper used in this book complies with the Permanent Paper Standard issued by the National Information Standards Organization (Z39.48–1984).

10 9 8 7 6 5 4 3 2 1

Copyright Acknowledgments

The author and publisher gratefully acknowledge permission for use of the following material:

Selected material from Gordon Arnold, "The Emergence of Faculty Unions at Flagship Public Universities in Southern New England," *Labor Studies Journal* 22, no. 4 (1988): 62-87 appears by permission of Transaction Publishers. Copyright © 1988 by Transaction Publishers; all rights reserved.

To Gregory and Jeffrey

Contents

Preface

The colleges and universities of the United States are a major resource, and higher education is sometimes regarded as an important growth industry in its own right. Higher education is called upon to do many things, of course, but its core activities of teaching and research rely on its faculties. What members of faculties do and how they do it are sources of debate and controversy, but there is no denying their centrality to the higher education enterprise. Yet our view of faculties is often one-dimensional. Depending on an individual's inclinations, members of the professoriate are either engaged in important work or else are self-absorbed freeloaders. The popular press has tended to stress the latter view, particularly in recent years, in books having provocative titles that sum up how many people regard higher education faculties. The titles of mass-market books such as *Tenured Radicals* and *Killing the Spirit* provide colorful evidence of the low regard in which much of society holds professors. Whatever one's inclinations, there could be no colleges and universities as we know them without the professoriate.

This book is about the process of unionization among university faculties. Faculty unions—whether of public school teachers or university professors—invite polemical musings. In higher education settings, faculty unions may have improved the situations of many faculties that adopted them. They may have accomplished this, however, at the cost of increasing public skepticism and, at times, antagonism.

Faculty unionization in public institutions is inevitably a political affair. Change in state entities could hardly be otherwise. It is not, however, random or haphazard. The lengthy process to secure a collective bargaining agent—in common language, to unionize—is often exhausting. It seldom, if ever, is undertaken on a whim. Unionization may offer the promise of improved working conditions and wages, but it may also exact a toll on the sometimes delicate balance of relationships among actors on a campus.

In this book, I have tried to write about unionization without casting the various factions as heroes or villains. In the three historical cases that form the core of the book, there are, of course, actions with which one might agree or disagree. In the heated debates that can arise during a unionization campaign, intemperate things can be said and sometimes done. To focus on these statements and actions as representative would be a mistake, however; such an approach would divert attention away from the importance of underlying political and economic forces that largely drove events. It is those broader themes, rather than the psychology of individual motivation, that inform the accounts that follow.

Acknowledgments

I am grateful to Clyde W. Barrow, Director of the Center for Policy Analysis at the University of Massachusetts at Darmouth for his interest in this project. The support of the Center was invaluable to this project, as was a sabbatical leave from Montserrat College of Art that made it possible to move the project forward. Ted I. K. Youn and several anonymous readers made helpful comments on various versions of this study. The research in this book was greatly facilitated by the help of many librarians. Of special help was Lisa Driscoll Tuite, Head Librarian at the *Boston Globe*, as were librarians and archivists at the University of Connecticut, the University of Massachusetts at Amherst, the University of Rhode Island, and the Providence Public Library. I am also grateful to Jane Garry and the staff at Greenwood for their work on this project. Finally, I offer special thanks to Kimberlee Arnold, who provided editorial advice and much encouragement throughout this project, and to Gregory Arnold and Jeffrey Arnold, who were helpful in many ways.

CHAPTER 1

Introduction

Looking at U.S. institutions of higher education in the mid–twentieth century, one might have speculated about many changes to come. It is unlikely, however, that the unionization of faculties in these institutions would have been among the changes contemplated. Yet, just as faculty unionism would spread through the ranks of public school teachers, so, too, would a similar impulse emerge among faculties at many campuses across the United States. In short order, many university faculties, particularly in the public sector, began to investigate unionization as a viable course of action that could improve their lot. This was uncharted territory, however. There was little in prior experience that paved the way for such developments.

Faculty unions, especially at the university level, have been controversial since their first appearance on the higher education scene. As a consequence, the rhetorical environment surrounding the matter frequently has been overheated. There have been many polemic pronouncements, representing strongly opposing viewpoints. This often has deflected attention away from investigation into the underlying circumstances and issues that prompted the emergence and spread of the phenomenon. Yet, the appearance of faculty unions was a significant development, not only for the institutions that grappled with the issue directly, but also for higher education generally. The questions raised by the rise of unionism are not only about unions and collective bargaining. Rather, they aim at the heart of the academic enterprise, questioning assumptions about the role of a faculty and about the distribution of resources and power within institutions of higher education. How and why the faculties at some public universities went about establishing unions is the topic of this book. Rising faculty unionism in higher education signaled a powerful challenge to many aspects of academic life. For the participants who were initially involved in the process of faculty unionization—and for the faculty, administrators and policymakers who have followed them—the question of whether or not a faculty should unionize was momentous. The decision to unionize, and therefore to adopt a collective bargaining relationship with an institution, was not an action that was taken lightly. The decision has implications that can extend far into the future. When adopted, faculty unionization can significantly redirect the trajectory of a faculty's relationship with its institution.

The economic, cultural, and political implications of unionization can be difficult to predict. This was especially evident in the first decade of the movement. Many underlying questions pertaining to institutional values and priorities were brought to the surface. In the case of public universities, particularly, political actors and the news media can exert influence from outside an institution, sometimes recasting the debate about faculty-institutional arrangements in unexpected ways. These are among the reasons that the union-organizing process among higher education faculties constitutes a complex phenomenon.

Sufficient time has passed that, in many cases, the existence, or nonexistence, of a faculty union on a given campus can be taken for granted. For campuses where unionization came early, the reasons and events that triggered it are fading into distant memory. The first appearance of unionism among university and other higher education faculties, however, was a startling development in the history of American higher education. It was a significant challenge to more than three centuries of tradition. Timeworn understandings between institutions of higher education and their faculties were questioned, and new conceptions of life in the academic workplace were asserted. With its gradual emergence in the mid-1960s and dramatic growth in the following decade, unionism among the professoriate was evidence of a major realignment occurring within the academic world.

These developments would have been difficult to foresee just a few years earlier. During the period leading up to the early 1960s, higher education had expanded on a scale that previously had not been imagined as the phenomenon of mass higher education led to a surge in student enrollments. With ever-increasing numbers of students, the demand for academic labor also increased dramatically. Numbering 196,000 in 1948, for example, the U.S. professoriate rose to 250,000 only nine years later in 1957.[1]

Given these changes, the early 1960s was, by many accounts, a golden era in U.S. higher education. Research dollars flowed freely, largely due to massive government expenditures that were outgrowths of Cold War competition with the Soviet bloc and of emerging patterns in government spending on social programs. Although the social turbulence that later came to characterize the decade was nascent, on campus the prospects for the future looked bright.[2] Professors seemed well poised to help lead the way for social and technological improvements in American society. The growth of higher education had already led to the ascension of the professoriate to new levels of power and influence within institutions of higher learning, in a phenomenon that Christopher Jencks and David Riesman famously called the "academic revolution."[3] Although higher education in the United States has never been without critics, in many respects the early 1960s was a shining moment. At that time, the jarring changes that were in store for many members of the professoriate were not yet evident.

Indeed, change was in the air. Scarcely a decade later, the feeling of optimism that had been found on many campuses had largely evaporated. A crisis of confidence in existing social institutions led to widespread re-examination of many aspects of social and economic life in the United States. Doubts about the lingering war in Vietnam, coupled with a general uneasiness with many then-recent changes in American society, generated a growing skepticism about whether existing social institutions were capable of resolving society's problems, which seemed numerous and, in many cases, intractable. Among the most highly visible arenas in which new ideas clashed with tradition were college and university campuses. An era of student protests had developed. Struggles against war and injustice, or at least against the status quo, came to characterize campus life in the national imagination, a perception that the mass media helped to make popular. To make matters worse, by the early 1970s strains emerged in the national economy. This development made it increasingly difficult for government at the federal and state levels to sustain the spending patterns that had become habitual. In the place of increasing resources and increased levels of confidence among the professoriate came a new era that, in the non-elite institutions of higher education especially, was marked by austerity and retrenchment. As a consequence, life on many university campuses in the 1970s was becoming markedly different from what could have been expected only ten years earlier.

With these altered circumstances, the future prospects for professors seemed dimmer. Budget cuts loomed; uncertainty increased. Many members of the professoriate began to question their relationships with the colleges and universities that employed them. In what seemed a surprising turn of events, professors for the first time seriously entertained the idea of organizing labor unions and seeking collective bargaining. In an earlier era, such ideas might have seemed absurd, but now the idea began to seem less extreme, particularly in the public sector.[4]

Still, it remained a deeply contested proposition. The application of a labor union model of organization to the situation of professional employees such as a university faculty contrasted with the major traditions of organized labor. In many respects, it was at odds with commonly held conceptions about the appropriate role and scope of labor unions. Both inside and outside the academy, many found it difficult to reconcile the seeming contradictions inherent in the notion that a professor also might be a union member. After all, the professors were among the most highly educated members of society, and they seemed to be at the opposite end of the employment spectrum from workers who had traditionally turned to the methods of organized labor. What is more, the legal environment had not been particularly conducive for union organizing among so-called professional employees in any context, and certainly not among university faculty. Such reservations found expression in many quarters, including the ranks of faculties.

The struggle to establish faculty unions in universities and colleges brought conflict. Amid the general social turbulence of the 1960s and 1970s in the United States, many academic leaders were unprepared for yet another change. Boards of trustees were especially skeptical of faculty unionization, and the administrations beneath them tended to have little more enthusiasm for the idea. Within faculties, too, solidarity about unionization was also not something that could be taken for granted. Even at campuses where unionism took a firm hold, there were faculty members who strongly disagreed with that course of action. Such cleavages were to be expected, of course, given the vastly different world views within faculties who came from different generations and different disciplinary traditions. Faculties have never been known for unanimity of opinion, but the thought of acting through unions, rather than as individual scholars, was very different from the traditional way of approaching the academic profession. To some it was disturbing.

The idea of faculty unions challenged many aspects of academic life. Yet, the putatively traditional ideas about the structure, goals and organization of American higher education institutions are themselves the products of a long evolution. Though surface features may have remained generally stable over long periods of time, the inner workings of American colleges and universities have been constantly changing as these organizations have adapted to greatly varying circumstances. Conceptions about the meaning and appropriate fixtures of faculty life have evolved over the course of more than 350 years.

By the post–Second World War era, ideas about faculty life had reached a highly elaborated form that was widely shared and accepted throughout most of the academy. How unions would coexist with these features, or whether they should, were unanswered questions. Consider the prominent example of academic tenure. This practice did not gain broad acceptance until well into the twentieth century, but it became a nearly universal feature across the spectrum of U.S. higher education by mid-century. Yet, tenure systems can afford those working under them an extraordinary degree of job security, particularly when compared to the much more tenuous situation of mainstream American workers.

With the advent of faculty unionism, therefore, some reckoning of how union arrangements were to exist in the face of them would be necessary. Then there was the matter of governance. Again, the case with faculties was atypical among the U.S. workforce. By the time that unionism in their ranks emerged, faculties had gained substantially in their influence over many institutional matters. This contrasted sharply with the lesser influence that most unionized workers (and many non-unionized workers) were apt to have experienced. In these and other respects, faculty employment presents an unusual case. If unions were to be added to the picture, it was unclear what the consequences would be.

How, then, should the phenomenon of faculty unionism be approached? Most obviously, unionism among any category of workers is usually fueled by economic and legal considerations. Regarding the latter, there must be a legal basis on which to form a union, which cannot be taken for granted. If law permits, then the unionization impulse can be, in the economic sense, a rational response to perceptions about the current or future state of an employment relationship. In circumstances where it is perceived that the individual has only a limited ability to negotiate desired compensation and working conditions, the lure of the potential power of collective negotiation can be great.

Unionism, from this perspective, is almost solely instrumental. Its relative attractiveness to employees lies in a calculation, however uncertain and informal, about whether or not one is likely to be better off with the union than without it. Unless one is willing to allow for extraordinary amounts of altruism, there is little doubt that a vote by employees to unionize means that the majority of those employees expect the delivery of real benefits. The expectation is that these will come about in the traditional areas subject to collective bargaining—namely, wages, working conditions and continuation of employment. In the cases examined in later chapters, these elements are amply evident.

In the drive toward unionization among a university faculty, however, economic and legal concerns, though important, do not reveal the whole story. The peculiarities of the academic profession (such as tenure, as previously noted) make unionism among this group a more complicated, multidimensional affair.

POLITICAL AND CULTURAL DIMENSIONS

Changes to the economic and legal aspects of faculty employment have implications that extend beyond that relatively narrow focus. Such changes raise questions about the interrelated political and cultural foundations of an academic institution. In terms of politics, one cannot view rising (or declining) faculty unionism without considering what this says about the distribution of power on a campus. For a union to achieve the desired economic and legal outcomes is, after all, to exert power.

Not surprisingly, faculty unionization is usually viewed with apprehension, if not outright distaste, by administrations and governing boards. Typically, the thought of losing any substantial perquisites of power and authority as the result of a transition to a unionized environment is anathema to them. As the truism suggests, those with power rarely relinquish it willingly. The unionization process is played as if it were a zero sum game: For one group to get power, another must lose it.

In playing the game, however, the struggle for power is often cloaked in ideological and moralistic rhetoric. Faculty unionization thus may be framed in such varying terms as public accountability, class identity, student welfare, or institutional failure. The unionization question can be framed in language that seems remote from the sometimes-simpler issues underlying a unionization bid, such as salary concerns. Once the issue is rhetorically enlarged, however, the positions taken by various actors may prove to be difficult to change. Compromise may be more difficult, and acrimony among the various factions may increase.

In American society, unions are seldom, if ever, viewed as benign entities. They represent a challenge to, or else an affirmation of, one's ideological convictions. A faculty union drive—like the unionization effort of almost any group—is apt to elicit strong and emotional responses, both from union advocates and opponents. Opinions about unions and organized labor may be subject to change, of course, but actors in a unionization process come to the table with pre-existing attitudes that may influence their perception of unfolding local events.

Accordingly, it is important to recognize the possibility that many opinions expressed during the process of unionization may originate from already formed ideas about organized labor. The rhetoric emerging from the process of unionization therefore may be less tightly connected to the existing circumstances than one might expect. In practice, confident pronouncements and predictions about what will happen if a union is adopted are made even when evidence is shaky or inconclusive. The point is that, especially among stakeholders, it is easy to lose focus of the circumstances at hand and instead veer into actions and statements that are related to one's already established feelings about the appropriateness or inappropriateness of various arrangements in management and labor issues.

More broadly, an understanding of faculty unionism requires that attention be directed toward the important cultural shifts that unionization and collective bargaining imply. Though often motivated by the prospect of achieving desired outcomes in compensation and other specific workplace issues, the act of establishing a union and engaging in collective bargaining creates additional changes within the culture of a university. Fundamental assumptions about what values are important within the university, about the status and prestige of various actors within it, and about what, if anything, holds it together can be called into question as changes are proposed to the status quo. Even if many actors come to believe that current employment arrangements no longer satisfy changed circumstances, the level of enthusiasm exhibited for the adoption of a union model of faculty organization can be quite variable.

The shifts in organizational culture that faculty unionization can bring may or may not be welcomed by faculties or administrations. A faculty union changes the nature of the legal relationship between faculty members and the universities that employ them and, therefore, between faculty and the administration. Employment relationships, which might have been quite individualistic in many respects and subject to various side arrangements and informal understandings, are suddenly legalistic to a degree often not experienced on campus previously. What is more, because a union is recognized as the sole bargaining agent for members of a unit, there are usually more intermediaries between the individual faculty member and the institution than was the case earlier. In sum, a formal bargaining arrangement is unlikely to have the same degree of flexibility than can be accommodated under less formal and legalistic conditions. On the informal level, too, relationships change. The contest involved in a unionization drive may take its toll. Many relationships after a union drive are simply not the same as before, whether or not the drive is successful. This prospect can be very disquieting to members of an academic community. It is not surprising to find that, during a union drive and in the aftermath, informal working and personal relationships, which may have been cordial and longstanding, can be seriously, and sometimes irreparably, strained.

THE HIERARCHY OF ACADEMIC INSTITUTIONS

The system of U.S. higher education is highly stratified. Among the most important ways in which institutions are categorized are the formal and informal rankings along the lines of prestige, reputation, and influence. Some prominent examples of this impulse are the Carnegie classification scheme of colleges or universities, or such popular ratings as those published annually by *U.S. News and World Report*. The relative merits of ranking colleges and universities may be debated endlessly but, as a practical matter, such ratings have entered the national consciousness. As a result, not all schools—and, therefore not all diplomas—are regarded as having the same currency. The national reputation and ranking of an institution attracts considerable attention.

It has often been observed that the faculty union movement has been less successful at those institutions at the highest levels of prestige and reputation than at institutions that have not reached those levels. Generally speaking, faculty unionization is not a phenomenon that has been associated with the likes of Harvard or Stanford.[5] This discrepancy in unionization activity calls attention to the differing characteristics of universities and colleges inhabiting the ranks of higher education institutions.

The various strata of higher education institutions—ranging from the prestigious and influential research universities to locally known two- and four-year colleges of modest aspirations—have some similarities. In many respects, however, they represent distinct realms that have characteristics and properties that differ from each other to a great extent. When examining unionism among higher education faculty, then, it is important to bear in mind that what holds true for one segment of the higher education world may have little, if any, application to other segments. Even the term "faculty" may be misleading, since it implies different things at different types of institutions. Though both having the same job title, the typical community college professor inhabits a very different world than does the state or, certainly, the private university professor. The organizations for which these individuals work are vastly different in purpose and scope, and the expectations and norms of a faculty career within each differ accordingly. Such distinctions, which may seem commonplace to those intimately acquainted with higher education, may be all but lost on observers from the outside, including some of those in the realms of politics and the news media.

In this highly stratified system, universities—and particularly those organizations designated as research universities—are located at the apex. Though community colleges, four-year colleges, and so-called "comprehensive" institutions (those offering baccalaureate and master's degrees primarily), are important in their own right, the emphases on advanced graduate training and research provide the research university with a distinctive role in the higher education pantheon. A high level of professionalization marks faculty culture at these institutions because of the great weight placed on the generation of new knowledge through research.[6] Though faculties throughout American higher education are expected to pursue ongoing scholarship, this emphasis is most intense at the university level.

Further stratification exists within this university segment. Those institutions regarded as "national" universities, with unquestionable claim to prestige and legitimacy, are at the top. Beneath them are many layers, ranging all the way to relatively weak and unknown universities, including some with a tenuous claim to the designation of "university." Most universities are somewhere in between.

Scholars in recent years have taken special note of the fact that organizations that are not at the highest levels within a field of similarly aimed organizations generally seek out ways to emulate their more prestigious counterparts.[7] Thus, even at respectable, mid-range universities, there is a likelihood that norms, beliefs, practices and routines prevalent among more prestigious institutions will find their way into the local scene.[8] The emphasis on research, which, as noted above, is now pervasive throughout U.S. higher education, was originally such a phenomenon. Indeed, the thorough acceptance of the research culture throughout the university segment of higher education, as well as throughout the higher education enterprise more generally, is one of the great success stories in the spread of organizational values and practices from the top of the hierarchy to those institutions below. What does this have to do with faculty unionism? In the university stratum of America higher education, faculty unionism seems at odds with well-established norms and practices. Whereas it is not uncommon for mid-range universities to seek out patterns of organization that will make them more like institutions with greater prestige, unionism appears, at first anyway, to be a force coming from exactly the opposite direction. Very few universities that would be considered among the top tier have unionized faculties. Thus, in the act of merely considering, let alone adopting, faculty unions as a mode of organization on a university campus, a very different impulse is at work than one might otherwise expect. It is not a movement that can be attributed to the sort of imitation often seen in the spread of practices from the top down.

PUBLIC AND PRIVATE UNIVERSITIES

One more distinction must be noted: the differing realms of public and private institutions. Despite sharing many characteristics, the public and private spheres of higher education differ in many significant respects. Importantly, private corporate organizations and the state are fundamentally different in conception, a fact that is especially evident in workplace and employment matters. The relationship between employer and employee differs dramatically when the employer is the state, rather than a private entity. These differences have significant implications for the course of any proposed unionization effort. Labor organization in any sphere involves interrelated and overlapping dimensions. The complexities inherent in public sector unionization, however, present some unique aspects, as is shown in the following chapters.

With this background, the main project of this book is to address issues revealed in case studies of faculty unionization at three public universities in southern New England. Other types of institutions could also be usefully studied, but the experiences of these three organizations and their faculties offer many glimpses into the circumstances and processes that can lead to faculty unionization. Some of the material in this study might be applied to other segments of American higher education or to other related settings, but the unionization of faculty in these institutions is examined here for its intrinsic interest and because of the importance of these institutions to their respective states.

The focus here on public universities also adds some important dimensions to the examination of faculty unionism: the involvement of state policymakers and officer holders; and the politics of public discourse. Because public universities are state entities, almost every arena of their activity is, by definition, a matter of public policy. What transpires within them is more directly connected to the public than is the case with private organizations. The fact that tax dollars are involved, to whatever extent, inevitably invites public attention.

Additionally, within state governments public institutions of higher education represent arenas in which various parties can play out political contests. Indeed, a long tradition of vacillating public perceptions about higher education generally, and the professoriate in particular, makes state institutions particularly appealing topics for politicians who can use various higher education issues for their own purposes. Higher education is no more immune to political attention than any other aspect of state activity. In a very real sense, the department of motor vehicles employee, the public works employee, and the state university college professor are all potential objects of public scrutiny and criticism. This contrasts sharply with the situation in private higher education, where much less information is apt to be made public and where there is somewhat less motivation for extensive external criticism.

All of this is also an invitation for attention from the news media. In continual search for events and stories that will capture public interest, every domain of state activity represents possibilities. Events on a campus may seem intrinsically interesting, so that they call attention to themselves. Or else lawmakers, public officials, or other constituencies may successfully draw media attention to some aspect of a public campus controversy that seems appealing to reporters and editorial writers. In the drive toward faculty unionization at a public university, the conflict that is almost certain to be created can provide a wealth of potential fodder for the media. Moreover, a public whose interest in some university matter has been aroused represents a potential constituency to which advocates of any position may appeal for support. Participants therefore may seek to secure the weight of public opinion for their position as they attempt to sway the outcome of an issue to their favor. In addition to other considerations, then, an examination of faculty union organizing at state institutions must also attend to the public discourse that can emerge around the issue and that may influence the course of those events.[9]

PUBLIC UNIVERSITIES IN SOUTHERN NEW ENGLAND

Public universities are a source of interest to a community much broader than the higher education community alone. These institutions can be especially important organizations in the political, social, and economic life of a state. Any inspection of them—and of public institutions of higher education generally—reveals that there are many points of interaction between the arena of state politics and an institution. Importantly, it has been within the public sector of American higher education that faculty unionism has found a fertile breeding ground. Indeed, the story of faculty unionism as a phenomenon would be a different and less compelling story were it not for the great inroads that the movement has made in the public sector.

In viewing the process of faculty unionization, perennial themes emerge that reach to the core of the higher education enterprise. Obviously, chief among these is the nature of the relationship between a faculty and its institution. In public higher education, added to these is an additional element: the state itself. In the cases recounted in later chapters, faculty unionization was a phenomenon that was inexorably linked to state politics. It is impossible to reach an understanding of the rise of faculty unionism on these campuses by looking only at the internal dynamics of those organizations. In academe, and especially in public higher education, it seems that all politics is not local. Although what happens within a university organization is an important part of the story at these institutions, the external events and political relationships were not merely backgrounds to unionization on campus, but rather integral parts of a common tapestry, woven together with local considerations.

This book is primarily concerned with faculty unionization at the flagship public universities of the three southern New England states: the Universities of Connecticut, Massachusetts and Rhode Island. In the 1960s, none of the faculties at these institutions were unionized; by the end of 1976, they all were. What, then, were the circumstances that led to this outcome? How did unionism emerge and progress?

A generation has passed since the advent of faculty unionism in higher education, and it is now possible to examine faculty unionization from the perspective of history. Major shifts in public higher education systems can be viewed as functions of the specific historical circumstances and conditions in which they occurred. In looking at faculty unionization, then, it is important to consider not only the specific events and conditions within universities where they were proposed, but also the surrounding economic and political milieu.

There are several reasons for the focus on the public universities of southern New England. Although these institutions are not representative of the picture nationally, there is something to be gained by examining the Connecticut, Rhode Island, and Massachusetts cases as a group. First, though they have clear differences, taken together these states largely share a regional identity. They share many important cultural, political and economic characteristics. The region is therefore intrinsically interesting. Second, the central role that higher education plays in the region makes an understanding of significant events in that realm important. Third, there is the situation of public higher education in this region, which has clearly been an enterprise of lesser stature there than has been true of the leading private institutions in these states.

The relationship between public and private higher education in southern New England has never been one of equals. The Land-Grant Act of 1862 (commonly known as the Morrill Act) eventually precipitated the creation of public institutions in Massachusetts in 1863, Connecticut in 1881, and Rhode Island in 1888. These were small and comparatively weak institutions, however. They joined a thoroughly established higher education landscape, populated with many fine institutions, including powerhouses such as Harvard (established in 1636), Yale (1701), and Brown (established in 1764 as Rhode Island College). Realistically, this meant that the public institutions in these states were, at the moment of their creation, relegated to a secondary existence. Though over time each of the public universities in these states has gained a measure of respect in its home state and even nationally, none has seriously challenged their older and more prestigious rivals in the popular imagination.

Still, although not as prestigious as their internationally known counterparts, they have proven to be important institutions in their home states. Over time, they have served many state residents and have secured a significant place in the higher education milieu. The connections that graduating students make with these organizations can be more than simply one of an alumni/ ae relationship, however, because a substantial number of their graduates remain in their home state after graduation and therefore join the electorate. In 1999, the University of Connecticut, for example, calculated that 95,000 of its alumni lived in the state. The presence of a large alumni/ae base such as this provides a significant and ready-made electoral base, the members of which are directly connected to, and likely harboring opinions about, that institution. It is difficult to gauge the likelihood that this alumni/ ae electorate can be sufficiently mobilized to affect state higher education policy outcomes. Still, the presence of alumni/ae among voters provides an established audience to which political elites, the news media, and sometimes members of the university community themselves can appeal. It can provide a reason to engage in public rhetoric about the events and conditions within the institutions. Though perhaps not at the top of the list during routine events, a primed audience stands ready when controversies erupt on public campuses.

These circumstances complicated the emergence and development of faculty unionism at the Universities of Connecticut, Massachusetts, and Rhode Island in the late 1960s and early 1970s. Although unionization is a phenomenon that is largely between workers and management (or, in educational settings, between faculties and administrations), these related elements affect the conditions under which that working relationship unfolds in the public sector. An understanding of them is helpful when approaching the faculty unionization story.

PLAN OF THE STUDY

In the following chapters, attention is thus directed both to internal situations and processes and to external pressures that impinged on the rise and development of faculty unionism. Before specifically examining faculty unionization at the Universities of Connecticut, Massachusetts and Rhode Island, Chapter 2 turns to a consideration of developments leading up to those events and to the immediate context in which they unfolded. Both the unique history of faculties within the development of higher education in the United States and the important changes to the legal environment relating to empowering employees to engage in collective bargaining are discussed.

Chapter 3 presents a brief overview of the emergence and course of the faculty union movement. By the end of the twentieth century, faculty unionization in U.S. higher education had passed through several stages. These were related to changes in the overall political and economic climate in the United States and also to changes within academe itself. In the first phase, the legal framework for collective bargaining among faculty emerged. The movement spread rapidly. The U.S. Supreme Court's *Yeshiva* decision, combined with a political climate influenced by Ronald Reagan's quelling of an air traffic controllers' strike, were factors in a slowdown in union organization among faculty. Finally, in the last decade of the twentieth century, some quarters of academe showed a new willingness to entertain unionization as a solution to various problems.

Chapter 4 recounts the story of faculty unionization at the University of Rhode Island. The faculty at Rhode Island moved the most swiftly in adopting a union and collective bargaining in a climate of economic uncertainty and upheaval in university governance. The most powerful newspaper in the state took a keen interest in the events involving faculty at the university, creating a complicated scenario in which the faculty initiative took place. In the next chapter, the rugged path to faculty unionization at the University of Massachusetts is reviewed. Of the three cases in this study, Massachusetts is unique in the respect that the faculty undertook an initial attempt at unionization that failed decisively. The influence of state politics was evident throughout, and the process threatened to divide the faculty. Within a few years, however, the matter was resurrected, and another acrimonious contest began.

In Chapter 5, the unionization of the University of Connecticut faculty is discussed. In Connecticut, the circumstances that would lead to unionization became evident before the faculty, as state employees, had been granted the right to form a union for collective bargaining. The deteriorating relationship between the faculty and the university, as well as the vagaries of state politics and the overall economic picture, are reviewed in relation to the eventual vote to establish a faculty union.

The study concludes with some observations about the relationship between faculties and universities and with possible implications for future developments.

NOTES

1. Theodore Caplow and Reece J. McGee, *The Academic Marketplace* (New York: Science Editions, 1961), 209.

2. See Ronald R. Johnstone, *The Scope of Faculty Collective Bargaining: An Analysis of Faculty Union Agreements at Four-Year Institutions of Higher Education* (Westport, CT: Greenwood Press, 1981).

3. Christopher Jencks and David Riesman, *The Academic Revolution* (New York: Doubleday, 1968).

4. The impulse toward unionism among university faculty had precedents, such as the unionization of the faculty in some community colleges in the mid-1960s. It might also be argued that a precedent is found in the unionization of public school teachers, a movement that only slightly predated faculty unionism in higher education. However, though they share the designation of "faculty," the worlds of the public

school teacher and that of university professor remain very different from one another.

5. With few exceptions, faculty unionism has generally been absent at such institutions to date.

6. It is true that, to an extent, this statement could be applied to faculty in the other strata of U.S. higher education. Generally, although pressure is most intense at the university level the expectations for the amount and quality of original research remain most intense for faculty members.

7. See, for example, Paul J. DiMaggio and Walter W. Powell, "The Iron Cage Revisited: Institutional Isomorphism and Collective Rationality in Organizational Fields," *American Sociological Review* 48 (1983): 147–60.

8. Recent scholars have called this "isomorphism," borrowing a term from biology, but the phenomenon has long been recognized. David Riesman, for example, wrote of a similar impulse. See David Riesman, "The Academic Procession," in *Constraint and Variety in American Education* (Garden City, NJ: Doubleday Anchor, 1958), 25–65.

9. Bok and Dunlop make the very useful point that the news media has been an important part of the history of labor organization in Derek C. Bok and John T. Dunlop, *Labor and the American Community* (New York: Simon and Schuster, 1970).

CHAPTER 2

Faculty and Labor

The emergence of unionism among university faculties could be approached from several perspectives. Within the community of readers having a special interest in higher education, there is sometimes a tendency to regard faculty almost entirely as a special class of employees, and often little effort is made to compare any meaningful aspects of faculty employment to the experience of other workers. In many respects, this is understandable. The everyday rhetorical environment still places academics in "ivory towers" and everyone else in the "real world." Such language conjures images of the professoriate as being remote from the world and engaging in esoteric and, in the popular imagination, sometimes laughable, studies about things of little concern to the ordinary person.

To the general population, basic elements of the faculty employment picture—such as academic tenure, academic freedom, teaching loads, and requirements for research and community service—may seem obscure, if not bizarre. For their part, academics have done little to explain their work experience to the public or to provide cogent arguments to the public as to why existing faculty employment arrangements are appropriate and should be continued. As a result, it has not been unusual to find faculties under pressure from the political realm, and sometimes from their own boards of trustees, to acquiesce to changes in their working arrangements. In the 1990s, for example, proposals to radically alter tenure at the University of Minnesota created a firestorm within faculty ranks and a threat to unionize. In another example, a powerful state higher education official in Massachusetts initiated a very public war against tenure at state institutions of higher education there during the same decade.

All of this heightens public perceptions of faculty employment as something that is unusual and privileged. It is certainly not a scenario in which faculties, at public institutions especially, can count on immediate public sympathy for maintaining the status quo in conditions of faculty employment. It seems evident that those outside the ranks of faculty often see the essential components of faculty work quite differently from the academics holding those positions. These conflicting perspectives and assumptions have the potential to significantly color relationships between faculties and their institutions. One cannot deny that many features of faculty work are in many ways unique. Understanding the nuances of faculty work is, therefore, an important part of understanding the emergence of unionism among faculty.

When faculties in higher education turned to unionism, they invoked a conceptual model that had little in common with the conception of a faculty as a rarified and privileged group. To the contrary, this was a move that highlighted an awareness that academics are, in fact, workers, even if atypical components characterized their employment arrangements. Thus, the emergence of faculty unionism made the connection between faculty employment and the broader realm of labor relations more explicit than before. It represented a major shift in the public view of faculty work.

The road to faculty unionism was long and winding. To understand how conditions were created that would be conducive to unionization, there are at least three strands of history that are important. As indicated above, the first and most obvious strand is found in the evolution of faculty work generally. This aspect of the story is deeply embedded within the development of higher education as an institution in American life. Second, developments in understandings about employment and labor on the American scene are essential to understanding the decision to pursue faculty unions. Third, there is the special case of public employees, whose relationship to their employers has substantive differences from their private sector counterparts. These are now discussed in turn.

FACULTIES AND THE ACADEMIC WORKPLACE

The conflicting perceptions of academic life often harbored by faculties and administrations have roots that reach deep into the history of American higher education. Over the course of that history, relationships among institutional actors were established through a long and continuing evolutionary process. As a result, ideas about the role, scope and requirements of faculty life have not been static. Many assumptions about the relationship between faculties and their employing institutions in the United States have changed dramatically over time.

In the few colleges of the English colonies, and later in the early years of the republic, college faculties comprised more generalists than specialists. They typically held little power or influence within their institutions, which were dominated by presidents and boards of trustees. The colleges themselves played only a marginal and peripheral role in society, and little concerned the average person. Usually sectarian, these small institutions were useful in training clergy, but the classical curriculum of the day had only a tenous connection to everyday experience. The economic role of the colleges was negligible, especially given that there were few, if any, ways of making a living—outside of the clergy—for which one would need a college education.

It is important to note that from their inception, the American colleges (and later universities) had never been modeled after an idealized collegium, in which a community of scholars would share authority and chart the course of the institution. Instead, reflecting the influence of English business practices, the colleges were created in the image of chartered corporations.[1] Thus, these early colleges adopted an organizational form in which lay boards held formal authority and, in concert with the institution's president, made all of the significant decisions.[2] The president's role was that of head administrator and head teacher. Other instructors were, in essence, the president's assistants.

As the republic grew in the nineteenth century, change slowly came to the colleges. The place of the college in society was debated. Although the older view of the curriculum was slow to change (a widely circulated report from Yale, for example, dampened enthusiasm for curricular innovation as early as 1828), faculties gradually began to play a more important role in some of the colleges. As more members of these faculties began to travel abroad, the influences of the European universities increased. The German university model held a particular fascination for American academics. In those organizations the culture of research and specialization predominated, and professors wielded real power. In the United States, through the nineteenth century, institutions of higher education had placed little emphasis on advanced learning. In fact, no U.S. institution had even awarded a Ph.D. until 1861.[3] After the Civil War, however, that situation changed abruptly as much of the emphasis in American higher education shifted from undergraduate to graduate education. The rapid success of upstart organizations such as Johns Hopkins University and Clark University, which were originally devoted entirely to graduate training, put pressure on the older institutions to place increased emphasis on advanced learning. In response, many of the older colleges grafted graduate schools onto their existing undergraduate programs, thus transforming colleges into universities. Not even the likes of Harvard or Yale could withstand the momentum of the university movement, and they, like so many other colleges, eventually were reconfigured as universities. Of course, as the prestige of universities rose, so too did the need for professors with advanced training to serve them.

The university movement was further fueled by the Morrill Act of 1862, in which funds from the sale of federal lands were used to finance higher education. One important result of this was the increasing appearance of public colleges and universities, in the modern sense. In some states, public institutions of higher learning were created in an environment with little competition, and eventually state-run universities would dominate the higher education scene within that jurisdiction. In other cases, including the New England states, the newly created public institutions were newcomers that shared the higher education landscape with institutions that, in some cases, already had long histories.

Though higher education was changing, until well into the twentieth century its main appeal was still to a relatively small segment of the population—one that primarily was elite, of European descent, and male. Nonetheless, the gradual, sometimes painstakingly slow, process that broadened the scope of higher education had begun. These developments planted the seeds for

a future in which higher education would come to play a much more central place in American society and would be available to a wider audience.

The rise of universities and the increasing visibility of institutions of higher learning in society led to a transformation of faculty in American institutions of higher learning. In many cases, the ways that faculty viewed themselves, and were viewed by others caring to look, changed significantly. In general, there was a new emphasis on graduate training and specialization. Consequently, the credentials of advanced training—especially the Ph.D.—were prized and eventually became the standard requirement for entry into a respectable faculty position. In the process, faculty members became certified experts, rather than the generalists of an earlier day. They became an elite class in their own right.[4]

These changes also led to a new fragmentation among faculties. They began to exert more control over the new disciplinary pantheon that emerged from the earlier generalized assortment of disciplines. With this came the establishment of disciplinary associations. As the disciplines coalesced, faculty members often came to believe that they had more in common with their disciplinary counterparts in other institutions than they did with fellow faculty members in different disciplines at their own institutions.

With the rise of universities from the late nineteenth century onward, organizational differentiation occurred rapidly and comprehensively across the spectrum of American higher education. The homogeneous world of early American higher education was replaced by an increasingly heterogeneous one, and it became highly stratified, as institutions of higher learning were arrayed in complex hierarchies of prestige and resources.[5]

Under these circumstances, not all faculties benefited equally. The increasing influence of faculty within the top tier of institutions was not representative of higher education faculty as a whole. Therefore, the character of faculty employment relationships could differ dramatically, depending on the employing institution. By the period following the Second World War, the power, influence and prestige of American faculty could be seen to vary substantially across institutional types.[6]

Higher education in the United States had changed significantly, and the new faculties of research scholars differed greatly from earlier generations. The structure of the relationship underlying the association between a faculty and an institution, though evolving, nonetheless retained important features from the earlier era. Although they had achieved elevated standing in some important respects, faculty members were clearly subordinate to the governing boards. Indeed, in many ways the governance patterns of the new public colleges and universities in the late nineteenth century were similar to their private counterparts, with the state (or an inferior body of it) playing the role of the corporate owner of the institution. The new higher education order that came about after the 1870s, therefore, had not immediately brought about greater job security for faculty. For faculty members who expressed views that contradicted those of board members or presidents, or who veered from the ideological mainstream, the threat of job loss was far from uncommon.

The gradual institutionalization of academic tenure in the next century changed that situation. With the acceptance of tenure and formalized understandings of academic freedom, job security for faculty was greatly enhanced. Over time, these elements came to be viewed as essential components of the employment relationship, at least from a faculty perspective. For those outside the academy, however, both tenure and academic freedom were curiosities that were only vaguely understood. For those who were antagonistic to the ideological leanings of the professoriate, these elements provided ready-made targets for allegations of abuse and unwarranted privilege. By the Cold War period, for example, policies of tenure and academic freedom could be portrayed as shielding leftward-leaning or rabble-rousing academics who, in other employment venues, would have been ousted from their positions.

The Rise of Professional Administration

The growth and success of universities, proffering a vision of higher education that stressed research and graduate training, had profound implications for the management of these institutions. The rise of managerial organization within universities and

colleges—with layers of vice-presidents, deans, chairs, and administrative officers—was a major development that altered the situation of faculties on campuses across the nation. In particular, the bureaucratization of the academy complicated the relationship between faculties and their institutions. With the delegation of responsibility and authority for many areas of campus life to professional administrators, the resulting fragmentation of decision making provided an arena for competition and sometimes conflict. The rise of management was not necessarily an entirely unwelcome development to faculties, however. On many campuses, especially where the research orientation was strong, the offloading of nonacademic aspects of faculty work could be welcome news to faculties, who sought more time for research. They were glad to be freed from what were sometimes viewed as mundane tasks associated with undergraduate life.

At the same time, however, the growth of an academic bureaucracy led to two changes that were sometimes problematic. First, with bureaucratized administrations came new wrinkles to the organizational culture. In administrative culture, power and authority tended to be vertically oriented. The major emphases were on institutional needs and efficacy. At first, when many administrative posts were filled by academics, these inconsistencies with academic culture did not necessarily create insurmountable differences between the two groups. Over time, however, as administrative specialists—rather than academics—came to fill many of those posts, the separation widened.[7] The accompanying attitudes of skepticism and the feelings of mutual alienation between the groups would be important elements in the later emergence of unionism among faculty.

Second, the rise of a professionalized faculty and a managerial bureaucracy also created organizations in which two decision-making structures coexisted.[8] Over time, the academic side and the managerial side of the operations could produce differing perceptions and norms in terms of what was right and appropriate within an academic community. Faculty and administrative personnel ostensibly exerted authority over different arenas. Faculties gradually gained significant control over curricular matters and over who would be hired to teach in the given disciplines, which were clear indications that their march toward a professional status had largely been successful.

Significantly, governing boards and administrators usually came to accept something resembling faculty sovereignty in such matters. The degree of specialization in most disciplines was so highly developed that those outside the disciplines arguably would have little basis on which to make many of these decisions. Still, on a formal basis, curricular decisions and hiring and promotion decisions made by faculty were usually advisory. Boards and administrators could, and at times did, decline to accept the "decisions" of faculties. When such disputes did occur, the underlying tensions between those holding formal authority and those holding academic expertise were quickly brought to the surface. Indeed, questions of decision and authority were often not clearcut in the complex organizations that universities, and many colleges, had become.

DEVELOPMENTS IN AMERICAN LABOR RELATIONS

A second strand of historical development relevant to the emergence of faculty unionism can be found in the more general history of labor in the United States. While faculty members are employees, modern college and university academics have tended to emphasize their claim to the status of professionals. Often, faculty members seem to hold the view that their relationship to employing institutions has little in common with that of the many other workers on the same campus. There is little evidence that faculties see their employment situation as comparable to the experiences of campus building and grounds workers or food service staff.

As noted above, faculties often do enjoy a certain degree of "shared governance" with the administration that other university employees do not. However, faculty members in many disciplines—particularly in the traditional arts and sciences—do not have a realistic opportunity to practice their professions outside of employing institutions. One cannot imagine, in any practical sense, most arts and sciences professors in private practice, and there is little demand for workers holding Ph.D. degrees with specialties in literature or philosophy in the business world, for example. Faculty members may be professionals, but they are not independent. In many respects, they constitute a category of workers that Gary Rhoades has aptly called "managed professionals."[9] Academics rely on colleges and universities to provide the essential venues in which they can practice their professions. They hold little formal authority over them, however. All of these considerations, which call attention to how faculties are located in the labor force, are important elements in an understanding of faculty unionism.

Many aspects of life in the United States have long been influenced by the hegemony of business interests.[10] Although examples of organized labor can be found dating far back in the nation's history, throughout much of that time their penetration into mainstream American thought and practice has been dubious. Organized labor has had some major successes. On balance, however, in the United States it can be argued that labor unions have not had consistent success in shaping the development of the world of work.

The instruments of government have traditionally been more closely allied with business and industry than with labor. Historically, the courts were not sympathetic to unions, and the Congress seldom dealt with labor-management issues at all, particularly before the 1930s.[11] Along with the sweeping changes wrought by the Great Depression and emergence of liberalism, however, came the Norris-LaGuardia Act of 1932.[12] This legislation looked favorably at union activity in a way that was a marked change from the past. For the first time, for example, Norris-LaGuardia placed some restraints on the judiciary in labor matters. Previously, the courts had been quite willing to issue injunctions against union activity, which obviously hindered the development of the labor movement. The act also declared that individual workers should have "full freedom of association, self-organization, and designation of representatives of his [sic] own choosing, to negotiate the terms and conditions of his [sic] employment."

Norris-LaGuardia established these principles, but it was the National Labor Relations Act of 1935 (known as the Wagner Act) that gave force to them. This new act specified several types of "unfair labor practices" that management was henceforth prohibited from undertaking, and it established majority rule as the principle for choosing a representative to bargain for employees. In addition, one of the most significant elements of the Wagner Act was the creation the National Labor Relations Board (NLRB), a federal agency with authority for sorting out the mechanics of organized labor in the private sector.[13] The NLRB was specifically authorized to administer union elections in the private sector and to consider unfair labor practices. It was further enabled to function in a somewhat judicial capacity through its ability to issue cease and desist orders and to order the reinstatement of employees.

The fact that federal legislation and NLRB jurisdiction applied only to the private sector was significant and is of fundamental importance in understanding the differences in patterns of faculty unionization in the public versus the private sectors. This difference between public and private employment in treatment under law stems from a tradition of viewing a public employer (ultimately, the state) as fundamentally different in nature from a private employer. Following eighteenth-century British tradition, this line of thinking draws a distinction between the state, which is a sovereign entity, and private employers, which clearly are not.[14] An important implication of this reasoning is that although the state cannot be required to enter into labor arrangements (i.e., collective bargaining), at the same time there is no prohibition from it doing so voluntarily.[15]

Overall, the Wagner Act was a significant advance for organized labor. Its enactment, occurring during the same period when public sympathy for unions had increased, created a climate for labor that had not been seen previously. During the Second World War, public support for unions and organized labor remained high, especially in light of organized labor's vow not to strike during the war so as not to undermine the war effort.

By the late 1940s, however, the situation changed. The Labor-Management Relations Act of 1947 (more commonly known as the Taft-Hartley Act) was enacted in response to assertions that the Wagner Act had tilted the balance between labor and management too much in labor's direction. Designed as a remedy for that perceived state of affairs, it established the principle that unfair labor practices could be applied to unions as well as management.

These and other changes were regarded as a setback by the labor community. All of these developments in the legal environment would prove important in establishing the framework in which faculty unionism was later to be played out, particularly at private institutions that were covered in federal legislation over the years. Yet, in many important respects, the faculty unionization movement in higher education was closely linked to developments in the public sector union movement. Though private, as well as public, higher education faculties have explored and adopted unionization, the original impetus for unions among these groups was largely linked to changes that came about in the public sector.

UNIONS AND PUBLIC EMPLOYMENT

Organized labor in the private sector made some advances over time, and became an important political force in many respects.[16] Less progress was forthcoming in the public sphere since, as noted above, the various branches of government could not be compelled to bargain with a union. Under these circumstances, it was not surprising that there was little activity on this front for many years. Even for union-minded workers, there seemed little hope that collective bargaining would be able to make consequential inroads in governmental workforces. At the state level, only Wisconsin, in 1959, specifically permitted its employees to engage in collective bargaining.

Changes at the federal level changed the situation in 1962. In that year, John F. Kennedy issued Executive Order 10988, which granted collective bargaining rights to federal employees of executive agencies.[17] Though a somewhat tentative first step, this action paved the way for a new way of thinking about public employees, whose numbers had been rising, making this sector a substantial proportion of the national workforce. Executive Order 10988 soon proved to be influential beyond the executive branch of the federal government and became a model for expanding labor organization rights among workers in many states.

The changing labor policies aimed at state and municipal workers varied widely across the states. The attitudes about an organized public workforce that were evident in the industrialized, labor-friendly states, often differed dramatically from those in states where organized labor in the private sector had failed to take hold. States in the former group (e.g., Connecticut, Massachusetts, Michigan, New York, Rhode Island, Wisconsin) tended to look more favorably on the idea of unionized public employees than did states where organized labor had a weaker presence. The states that adopted statutes granting collective bargaining rights to public employees often followed the federal model in establishing a state entity more or less in the image of the NLRB, which continued to have no jurisdiction over public employment matters. Such specific mechanisms to deal with state and local level collective bargaining were slower to develop elsewhere.[18]

There were differences not only in where public-employee collective bargaining rights were granted among the states, but also in the details specifying the particular arrangements even where such rights were granted. Which employees would be covered under such plans was one question. Other issues related to the practices that would be permitted. For example, even in a labor-friendly state, it remained uncommon to find a willingness to allow strikes by public employees. Some states, moreover, restricted what employment matters would be permissible topics for collective negotiations. One such state was Massachusetts, which at first did not allow bargaining on the issue of wages. (This was later changed.) The exact articulation of who would be covered, what practices would be allowed, and what could be negotiated together created a milieu in which public employees might or might not judge unionization to be attractive as a means of bettering their working arrangements.

Public and Private Employee Union Participation

An examination of patterns that emerged in union participation among the workforce over the course of the developments noted above is revealing. In 1930, prior to Norris-LaGuardia, union membership accounted for only 11.6 percent of the American workforce. A decade later, this had risen dramatically to almost 26.9 percent. What is more, the Bureau of Labor Statistics reported that this percentage rose to over 30 percent union membership in each of the years that were reported between 1945 and 1960. After this time, however, there was a steady decline in the percentage of overall union membership in the labor force. By 1994, for example, only 15.5 percent of the total labor force could be counted as members of unions or other organizations that engaged in collective bargaining with employers. Overall, the zenith of organized labor seemed to have occurred before the 1970s. This is underscored in public opinion polls from this period, which consistently revealed that a substantial segment of the public harbored skepticism about unions. For example, polls conducted by the National Opinion Research Center between 1973 and 1989 showed that the percentage of respondents who reported "a great deal" of confidence in labor unions never rose to more than 20 percent.[19] At the same time, the percentage of respondents who expressed "hardly any" confidence in labor unions was never less than 27 percent.[20] Often, the figures were higher, as in 1986, when it was 42 percent.[21]

The emergence of college and university faculty unions during roughly this same period, when union membership across the labor force was in decline, is therefore an interesting phenomenon when compared to the whole of labor history. If the public segment of the labor force is treated separately, however, a very different picture emerges. It is important to keep in mind the enormous growth of public sector employment in the post–World War II period, which had reached a level of one of every five employed persons by 1977.[22] Although the proportion of private-sector workers who were union members was declining during this time, the public-sector unionization movement had gathered force. By 1975, a third of public sector employees were organized, making it arguably the most vital element in organized labor at that moment and for some time to come.[23] Indeed, in the decade from 1965 to 1975, three unions—the American Federation of Teachers (AFT), the American Federation of State, County and Municipal Employees (AFSCME), and the American Federation of Government Employees—managed to double their memberships by concentrating almost entirely on public sector organization.[24] It was within this context that faculty unionism at all levels came about. As shown in the following chapter, the stunning success of the AFT and other teachers' unions would have particular consequences for a similar impulse among college and university professors.

Public-Employee Bargaining in Southern New England

As an industrialized region, organized labor has been well established in southern New England. Labor unions have been part of the scene for a long period and, generally speaking, labor unions seem broadly, though not universally, accepted there. Added to this is the traditional strength of the Democratic Party, which has historically been sympathetic to labor. As a consequence, a legal environment developed that was conducive to state-employee collective bargaining. Although coming about at different speeds, by the mid-1970s, each of these states had granted broadly conceived rights to its public workers.

The case of Massachusetts is a useful illustration, not unlike its neighbors in spirit. The underlying philosophy toward collective bargaining in the workforce is expressed in Chapter 150A of the Massachusetts General Laws:

It is hereby declared to be the policy of the Commonwealth to eliminate the causes of certain substantial obstructions to the free flow of industry and trade and to mitigate and eliminate these obstructions when they have occurred by encouraging the practice and procedure of collective bargaining.

More specifically, the collective bargaining rights of public employees in Massachusetts are specifically treated in Chapter 150E, which states:

[Public] Employees shall have the right of self-organization and the right to form, join, or assist any employee organization for the purpose of bargaining collectively . . . and to engage in lawful, concerted activities for the purpose of collective bargaining or other mutual aid or protection.

The situation in Rhode Island has been similar. Legislation enacted in 1966 was comprehensive and permitted organization by state employees for the purpose of collective bargaining on a broad basis. In fact, the law in Rhode Island was probably the least ambiguous of the laws in the three states in many respects, and its early passage was undoubtedly one reason that University of Rhode Island faculty chose the collective bargaining route as early as 1971. In Connecticut, the road to a legal environment that would permit faculty in public colleges and universities to organize was more winding. Legislation was attempted for public employee bargaining rights several times from 1970, but it was not until 1975, when the Democrats regained control of the governor's office, that enabling legislation was signed into law.

CONCLUSION

These developments would soon come together to produce a vigorous faculty union movement in American higher education. As new challenges were directed to academic work, some members of the professoriate looked outside academe for models on which to reconstruct the relationship between faculties and administrations. This connected unionist activity among faculties to the broader traditions in American labor history. The changing direction of labor relations between the government and its employees fleshed out the possibilities and provided the foundation for union organizing activities among faculties.

At the end of the day, unionization of the academic rank and file would not be universal. Union organizing among the faculties of private universities and colleges would fail to match the success in the public sector. Nor would the movement make significant headway in organizing faculties at elite institutions. Over its first decades, the faculty union movement has taken many twists and turns. We next turn to a brief overview of the movement as it played out in its first three decades, of which the faculty-unionization stories at the Universities of Rhode Island, Massachusetts and Connecticut are part.

NOTES

1. See E. D. Duryea, "Evolution of University Organization," in

ASHE Reader on Organization and Governance in Higher Education, ed. Marvin W. Peterson (Needham Heights, MA: Ginn Press, 1988), 165–82.

2. Ibid.

3. Frederick S. Rudolph, *The American College and University: A History* (New York: Alfred A. Knopf, 1962), 269.

4. See Laurence R. Veysey, *The Emergence of the American University* (Chicago: University of Chicago Press, 1965).

5. The Carnegie classification of institutions is one such way of looking at this sphere of education that clusters institutions with similarities in educational programs as well as a de facto organization along resource-availability lines.

6. See Jencks and Riesman, *The Academic Revolution.*

7. See Johnstone.

8. See Robert Birnbaum, *How Colleges Work: The Cybernetics of Academic Organization and Leadership* (San Francisco: Jossey-Bass, 1988).

9. See Gary Rhoades, *Managed Professionals: Unionized Faculty and Restructuring Academic Labor* (Albany: State University of New York Press, 1998). Rhoades makes many useful points in his discussion of the employment status of faculties in American higher education.

10. For commentary on the influence of business interests, see Charles S. Lindblom, *Inquiry and Change: The Troubled Attempt to Understand and Shape Society* (New Haven: Yale University Press, 1990).

11. Arthur S. Sloane and Fred Witney, *Labor Relations,* 6th ed. (Englewood Cliffs, NJ: Prentice Hall, 1988), 98.

12. See Theda Skocpol and Kenneth Finegold, "Explaining New Deal Labor Policy," *American Political Science Review* 84 (1990): 1297–1315.

13. See Sloane and Whitney.

14. Bok and Dunlop, 322.

15. Ibid.

16. See Edward O. Laumann and David Knoke, *The Organizational State,* Madison: University of Wisconsin Press, 1987.

17. Sloane and Witney, 35, 37

18. Bok and Dunlop, 321.

19. Floris W. Wood, ed. *An American Profile: Opinions and Behavior, 1972-1989* (Detroit: Gale Research, 1990), 668.

20. Ibid.

21. Ibid.

22. Michael A. Mass and Anita F. Gottlieb, "Federally Legislated Collective Bargaining for State and Local Government," in *Labor Relations in the Public Sector: Readings and Cases,* 2d ed., ed. Marvin J. Levine (Columbus, OH: Publishing Horizons, 1985), 77.

23. Charles Redenius, "Public Employees: A Survey of Some Critical Problems on the Frontier of Collective Bargaining," in *Labor Relations in the Public Sector: Readings and Cases*, 2d ed., ed. Marvin J. Levine (Columbus, OH: Publishing Horizons, 1985), 7.

24. Mass and Gottlieb, 78.

CHAPTER 3

Three Decades
of Faculty Unionism

Looking at the course of faculty unionism in American higher education from its abrupt appearance in the mid-1960s until the end of the twentieth century, one can see ebbs and flows of the movement. In one sense, faculty unionization is a local event for a faculty and an institution, and each case presents nuances and circumstances that are unique to that time and setting. This chapter, however, takes a different perspective. It briefly considers faculty unionization as a wider phenomenon—a movement, of sorts, consisting of an interconnected set of situations responding, on some levels, to broader social forces.

Faculty unions and collective bargaining have been on the scene in American higher education for only a short time. Still, it is possible to see in that short history several stages of development. Broadly speaking, three phases seem evident. First, there was an early period of intense activity, as the legal environment cleared and as unionism rapidly gained some measure of legitimacy in the higher education community. Second, there was a slowdown in the movement, which occurred as a result of the Supreme Court's *Yeshiva* decision in 1980, but which also was accompanied by societal and economic changes. By the latter half of the 1990s, a tentative new phase began as an increased willingness to explore unionization seemed to emerge, with the possibility that the movement would take on new life. These developments are summarized below.

NATIONAL ORGANIZATIONS AND THEIR ROLE

One important element of the faculty unionization movement has been the participation of national organizations active in unionizing activities. Indeed, the early and dramatic successes in unionizing faculties in both four-year and two-year institutions were greatly facilitated by the existence and efforts of these groups. The three major players involved in the effort have been the American Federation of Teachers (AFT), the National Education Association (NEA), and the American Association of University Professors (AAUP).

Very few college or university faculties have unionized without the participation of one of these faculty organizations. The encouragement, resources, and expertise that have been made available to faculties from these groups have enhanced local possibilities significantly. The rapid emergence of enabling legislation generated a unionist impulse on public campuses. Despite this new legal status, however, administrations and boards tended to prefer no union. It was not unusual, especially in the earliest phase, to find boards seeking to delay organizing efforts through various legal channels. In such cases, institutional resources—such as time, personnel, and money—typically dwarf the capabilities of local faculty groups to prepare a response. The national organizations leveled the playing field, or, from an alternate point of view, may on occasion have tipped the balance in favor of the faculty.

Of the three major players, only the American Federation of Teachers is a labor union in the traditional sense. Established in 1916, its labor pedigree is evident in its original ties to the American Federation of Labor and later to the merged AFL-CIO. As its name implies, its primary orientation has been directed at teachers in the public schools. However, during much of its early history, the AFT and its membership were engaged in social issues, sometimes from a radical perspective. As a result, throughout its history it attracted some members from higher education faculties who were drawn to its focus on the social and political agenda.

In 1961, the AFT achieved a major success in New York City, where its affiliate, the United Federation of Teachers, won a collective bargaining election. Building on this development, the organization was successful in gaining collective-bargaining representation rights for teachers in many jurisdictions. It sometimes reinforced its negotiating prowess by supporting teacher strikes.

Following its successes among rank and file teachers, the United Federation of College Teachers, local 1460, was organized in New York City in 1963. Within three years, the AFT's national office followed suit and established a separate college and university department, which promptly engaged in organizing higher education faculties.

Although not a universal tendency, faculties at two-year colleges have proven to be a major constituency of the AFT. The organization's ties to the K-12 schools have provided a natural bridge to faculties at the two-year colleges, which themselves have had some elements in common with the world of public school teaching. The structure of two-year faculty work, which has generally been teaching-focused rather than research-focused, is often seen as analogous to teaching at the so-called "lower" levels.

Still, the faculties of some four-year institutions have chosen the AFT as their bargaining agent as well. In the early years of faculty unionism, the group had notable victories at institutions such as Southeastern Massachusetts University (since merged into the University of Massachusetts system) in 1969. In another situation, the merger of two faculty units brought local affiliates of the AFT and the NEA together in a combined entity to represent faculty at the City University of New York and the State University of New York.

In general, the AFT has been regarded as the most "militant" of the three organizations. Its formal relationship to labor, which it proudly embraces, have perhaps served to perpetuate this view. These ties, and the criticism that the organization is dominated by the interests of public school educators, sometimes have been used by representatives of the other groups as evidence that the AFT has been insufficiently oriented toward higher education issues.

By contrast, the National Education Association has emphasized its identity as an association, rather than a traditional union. For many years after its founding in 1857, that was an accurate description. Its primary goal was to advance education and the teaching profession generally. The NEA did establish a higher education department in 1870. It remained active for the next five decades, after which it drifted from view. Although the higher education department was reactivated in 1943, its purpose remained one of professional enhancement and not labor organization.

With the AFT's rise as a collective bargaining agent in the 1960s, the NEA quickly followed suit. Although the NEA retained its traditional name, which identified it as an association, it soon came to function as if it were a labor union. It became deeply involved in organizing teachers for collective bargaining and in effectively promoting *de facto* strikes to achieve its ends.[1]

The NEA investigated the possibility of organizing higher education faculties as early as 1968. Upon study and consideration, the leadership of the organization decided to enter that arena, with the notion that its higher education department, the American Association of Higher Education (AAHE), would lead those efforts. The leaders of the AAHE, however, objected to the idea of unionizing college and university faculties and therefore declined to accept that task. In response, the NEA formed a new unit, the National Society of Professors, to lead its higher education organizing efforts. (It was not long before the AAHE separated from the NEA and became a freestanding organization.)[2]

The NEA was willing to work with other organizations to advance its objectives. Sometimes, the NEA worked closely with the AFT. (There was often talk of a formal merger between the two groups.) Later, in the 1970s, the NEA entered into an association with the American Federation of State, County and Municipal Employees, which was expanding swiftly as more states enacted legislation permitting collective bargaining by their public employees.[3]

With its enormous membership base, primarily of public school educators, the NEA has developed into an effective political entity. Seen as less militant than the AFT, it has been able to appeal to higher education faculties based on its strength, on the one hand, and its professional association identity, on the other.

The American Association of University Professors also avoided identification as a labor union. Founded in 1915, it spent most of its history explicitly rejecting a trade union model for faculty-institutional arrangements. The group discussed the possibility of adopting a union stance only a few years after its establishment. As early as 1919, however, AAUP president Arthur Lovejoy made the case that university faculties would be better served if they were "organized in an independent professional body, rather than as part of a national federation of labor unions."[4]

The AAUP has a long history of addressing issues that are usually identified as central to the academic profession. Its first major cause was that of academic freedom, a topic on which it has worked tirelessly for many decades. Tenure was also an important area for the group, and in 1940 it issued the first version of its well-known *Statement on Principles and Interpretative Comments on Academic Freedom and Tenure*. These facets of AAUP's work have played a significant role in guiding policy discussions on these and related topics in much of American higher education.

In the 1950s, the AAUP instituted its famous salary survey, which made it possible for faculties to compare their earnings with those of their peers at other institutions. Certainly the availability of this information was eye opening to many members of the professoriate. The survey data could be a source of contentment or unhappiness, of course, depending on how one's institution fared in the comparison.

The AFT and NEA were already fully engaged in organizing higher education faculties when the AAUP finally joined their ranks in 1972. At its annual meeting that year, its members resoundingly voted to embrace collective bargaining as a means of achieving its long-established ends. Although the vote on the issue was a landslide, there was fallout from the decision. Many members were prompted to leave the association. With about 97,000 members before the vote on collective bargaining, that number dropped by 10,000 in a year's time.[5]

The AAUP was substantially newer at the game of faculty organizing than either the AFT or the NEA, but in some ways it had an advantage, at least on some campuses. Its orientation, largely geared toward university faculties, and its reputation in working solely on higher education issues, appealed to the professional instincts of many faculty members, who sometimes had difficulty identifying with the other organizations and their K-12 teacher orientation. Moreover, with only higher education faculties to serve, the AAUP could argue that only it, of the three major organizations, could devote all of its attention to issues confronting college and university faculties. Its attention and loyalties were not divided.

The NEA and AFT responded to this claim. They argued that although engaged in activities covering the whole of teaching professions, their enormous bases of support among public school teachers lent an undeniable clout when dealing with governmental entities. This competitive theme among the organizations would play out on many campuses. In organizing drives, two, or perhaps all three, of these groups would vie for the right to represent college and university faculties in collective bargaining.

THE SPREAD OF FACULTY UNIONISM

From modest beginnings at just a few institutions in the mid-1960s, the faculty union movement spread swiftly. One could make the case that faculty unionism was a movement that spread from public school teachers to two-year colleges and then up through the ranks of four-year colleges and universities. There is some merit to this view, though it oversimplifies the process through which the faculties at individual institutions made the choice to unionize. It is true, however, that collective bargaining in higher education first appeared in the two-year college setting, at institutions such as Milwaukee Technical Institute, where collective bargaining was adopted in 1963.[6]

It can also be said that, to a great extent, faculty unionization has been a phenomenon of the public sector. This is consistent with the movement's successes at two-year institutions, an overwhelming number of which are public institutions, but it holds for four-year institutions as well. Once installed in public two-year colleges, it often has been a relatively short step to the four-year institutions in the same jurisdiction, though it has not always worked in this way. Yet, faculty collective bargaining was not confined to the public sector, even at the beginning. Some early campuses that adopted faculty collective bargaining were private institutions. One such case was Bryant College of Business Administration in Rhode Island, at which the faculty unionized in 1967.[7] This was the first case of faculty unionization at a traditional four-year institution. (It had been preceded a year earlier by the somewhat atypical U.S. Merchant Marine Academy.)[8]

As noted earlier, the presence of enabling legislation was instrumental in the rise of faculty unions. At about the same time, economic changes also became evident. The shrinking buying power of the dollar provided powerful fuel to the faculty union movement. The Consumer Price Index, for example, had risen at a relatively modest rate for several decades. In 1950, the CPI for all urban consumers was 24.1. It rose to 29.6 in 1960, followed by a somewhat sharper increase by 1970, when it was 38.8. In the 1970s, however, inflationary pressures increased enormously. In the decade after 1970, the CPI more than doubled, reaching 82.4 in 1980.[9]

In the short period between 1966 and 1974, faculty unionization in higher education made dramatic gains. Even if one does not include two-year institutions, the rate of growth was impressive. In 1966, only one four-year institution was unionized (the U.S. Merchant Marine Academy). The following year, the addition of Bryant College increased that number to 2. From that time, however, the ranks of organized four-year institutions grew rapidly. The total reached 40 four-year institutions in 1970 and 132 four-year institutions by 1974.[10] The number of professors who were included in collective bargaining units rose at an even quicker pace. From only 300 faculty members in 1967, this number had increased to over 60,000 only seven years later.[11] Momentum continued for several years, and by the end of the 1970s the number of four-year institutions (some with multiple campuses) with unionized faculties exceeded 250.[12]

The organizational environment had an effect on where unions were adopted, as mentioned earlier, with elite universities and colleges usually proving less conducive to the emergence of strong unionist leanings among faculties. Where collective bargaining was adopted, it tended to take one of two broad forms. The more "industrial" form, in which a management and workers are cast as adversaries, tended to appear where the balance of power had been skewed decidedly toward the administration and where the faculty was therefore weaker. Unions favoring an approach of cooperation and collegiality with administration were seen at institutions where existing arrangements and structures (such as faculty senates) had worked more effectively in addressing academic and professional issues.[13]

In its early years, faculty unionism attracted much attention from the higher education community. It was a novelty, but it seemed threatening to most academic leaders. Higher education researchers wanted to know why faculties joined unions, who among them were most likely to harbor union sympathies, and what the long-term effects of unions would be. In a study prepared for the Carnegie Commission on Higher Education, for example, Everett Carll Ladd, Jr. and Seymour Martin Lipset concluded that individual ideology played a large part in determining who would be sympathetic to the union cause.[14] Among the other important determinants, however, Ladd and Lipsett concluded that professors of "low scholarly achievement give greater backing to the principles of collective bargaining."[15]

Such observations helped emphasize the prevailing view that American higher education was a meritocracy, and that unionist impulses were the result, at least in part, of professors who could not compete with their elite peers. With the imprimatur of the Carnegie Commission, such conclusions certainly played a part in reinforcing a climate in which university and college leaders viewed faculty unionization as a setback for their institutions. Many mid-range institutions—the formerly modest colleges that had been transformed into state universities and comprehensive colleges—had newly arrived at their elevated positions in the higher education landscape, and their claims to a higher status remained tenuous. The administrators of such institutions surely recognized that the arrival of a faculty union would not enhance their prestige.

The growth of faculty unions met with some skepticism in the press, which in previous years had often exhibited a willingness to portray academics in a less-than-positive light.[16] A 1976 story in the *New York Times*, for example, stated that academics were "accustomed to looking with disdain at those who earn their living with muscles rather than their minds." It was these same academics, according to the story, who often behaved selfishly but were nonetheless protected by unions. The story concluded that "A faculty union . . . has been a principal party in the financial crisis that forced the City University of New York to close last week for lack of money" and that "Students, who have the most at stake, often are ignored as unionization proceeds."[17]

Though seemingly a potent force in the academic world, the rapid growth of faculty unions was not assured of continuing. The societal conditions that created the milieu in which unionization succeeded were subject to change. The emergence of faculty unions as powerful voices on some campuses and in some states also had a cost. Particularly at public institutions, union effectiveness could be seen as abrasiveness, and it was doubtful that support among the general population was very strong or deep.

Still, it was not uncommon in the 1970s for writers on the subject of higher education to envision a world in which faculty unions would continue to spread across the pantheon of American colleges and universities. A decade later, the movement would significantly slow down. In fact, it almost would come to a halt.

THE *YESHIVA* DECISION

The critical event in dampening faculty unionization in American higher education was the landmark 1980 Supreme Court decision in *National Labor Relations Board v. Yeshiva University*. For a decade prior to that decision, the NLRB had facilitated the organization of faculty unions at private institutions by approving bargaining-unit eligibility and conducting collective bargaining elections. When faculty unionism came to Yeshiva University, that institution did not accept the authority of the NLRB in the matter. The basic contention was that members of the faculty had significant managerial authority and responsibilities, and that they should therefore not be considered eligible for collective bargaining under provisions of the National Labor Relations Act. Although it had been very common for institutions to challenge the right of certain faculty members to be included in bargaining units, previously this had been confined primarily to faculty members serving as department chairs or as directors. What was different in the *Yeshiva* case, then, was that the claim of exemption due to managerial status was extended to include the entire faculty.

In a 5–4 decision, the Supreme Court ruled against the NRLB. The decision held that faculty members at Yeshiva University were essentially managerial employees and were therefore not covered under provisions of the National Labor Relations Act. It was the view of the court that the Yeshiva faculty exerted "absolute" power in academic matters and that it had "professional interests [that] . . . could not be separated from those of the institution."[18] In describing the extent of faculty authority, Justice Powell wrote:

They [the faculty] decide what courses will be offered, when they will be scheduled and to whom they will be taught. They debate and determine teaching methods, grading policies, and matriculation standards. They effectively decide which students will be admitted, retained and graduated.[19]

The *Yeshiva* decision was immediately controversial among members and observers of the higher education community. Critics of faculty unions hailed the decision, while supporters of collective bargaining among higher education faculties deplored it. Debate on the decision has raged for two decades.

Discussions about *Yeshiva* were often abstract, but the effects of the decision were quite real. In the private sector of higher education, the decision brought a virtual halt to organizing activities in its aftermath. Administrations and boards had never been enthusiastic about the advent of faculty unionization, and now the court supported that view. Within a few years, more than a dozen private institutions used *Yeshiva* as a basis to decline bargaining collectively with faculty.[20] By 1985, more than fifty such claims using *Yeshiva* as the basis were filed, and usually upheld.[21]

One celebrated event that also had a disquieting effect on supporters of faculty unions occurred at Boston University. Following on the heels of *Yeshiva*, that institution's president, John Silber, successfully fought to decertify the faculty union. The acrimony that surrounded this development lingered on the Boston University campus for some time, and it served as a chilling reminder to union-minded people elsewhere of the precarious situation of even already-existing bargaining units.

A LONG DROUGHT

The *Yeshiva* decision was not the only factor that exerted influence on faculty unions. By the era of Ronald Reagan's presidency, there were major shifts in the political and economic landscapes. It was not a particularly shining moment for organized labor. A strike by thousands of air traffic controllers in 1981, for example, gained substantial attention. The hard line taken by the Reagan administration in this case—11,000 members of the Professional Air Traffic Controllers Organization were subsequently terminated and the union decertified—cooled the environment for organized labor.[22]

There were also other changes. With an increasing number of Reagan appointees serving on the NLRB, that body seemed far less hospitable to would-be organizers.[23] The mood of the country had shifted and, coupled with the devastating effect of *Yeshiva*, organizing activities came to a virtual halt in private-sector colleges and universities. Even in the public sector, *Yeshiva* seemed poised to exert a chilling influence over the fate of legislative initiatives that would further extend organizing rights to faculties of public institutions.

By the 1990s, it was widely believed that the influence of faculty unions had sharply declined. For more than ten years after *Yeshiva*, successes in organizing new faculties were almost nonexistent. One exception involved the faculty of the University of New Hampshire. Although it had rejected collective bargaining in the 1970s, the faculty at New Hampshire reversed itself and voted to unionize in 1990. In the 1970s that would have been an unremarkable event. In 1990, it was reported to be the first time since 1986 that the faculty of a four-year institution had unionized anywhere in the United States.[24]

Indeed, throughout this period there seemed to be little point in beginning any unionizing activity on private campuses. It was clear that the NLRB would broadly apply the *Yeshiva* principles to private colleges and universities. A narrower application of *Yeshiva* seemed possible, of course, since not all faculties seemed to possess the characteristics of authority in the way that the Court had found was the situation at Yeshiva University. However, the nearly universal spread of shared governance in colleges and universities meant this would be difficult to prove. In any case, there was scant evidence that the NLRB had an inclination to press the issue on any more than an extremely occasional basis. For their part, the AFT, the NEA, and the AAUP, though unhappy with the status quo, had little reason to hope for a change anytime soon.

Even if they could successfully convince the NLRB to rethink the application of *Yeshiva*, there was still the substantial hurdle of the Supreme Court. It remained possible for a private institution to voluntarily agree to collective bargaining with its faculty, but this also was rare. There was also nothing in *Yeshiva* that prevented further organizing activities at public institutions, where state law permitted that, since the National Labor Relations Act does not apply to state employees. By the 1980s, however, most of the public-university faculties who wanted to organize and were permitted to do so had already taken some action. Few new states were interested in extending bargaining rights. More than decade after *Yeshiva* there were seventeen states that continued to prohibit unionization among public agency workers.[25] By this time, those states with an inclination to support public-employee organizing rights had already done so.

As the 1990s began, the situation was largely unchanged. Although the national faculty organizations hoped for a new beginning, there were few indications that major changes were imminent. This did not mean that organizing activities on campuses had ceased completely, but often it was not the full-time faculty that was the object of organizers. In tandem with the emergence of faculty unions some years earlier, there had been less visible efforts to organize graduate students. At institutions such as Yale University, graduate students pushed forward with their efforts to win recognition, often over the objections of faculty. There were also increased efforts to organize part-time faculty members.

Still, when the Democrats took control of the White House in the early 1990s, organized labor and faculty-union advocates were hoping for a more favorable political environment. In the private sector, it was a time of prosperity, and organized labor did show some signs of recovery. A change in direction for faculty-unionizing activity was more difficult to achieve, however.

By this time, faculty unions at the public school level were a popular target of politicians. During the 1996 presidential campaign, for example, one prominent theme of Republican candidate Bob Dole was his promise to fight the influence of teachers' unions. Although faculty unions in higher education were not singled out to the same degree in the campaign rhetoric, surely there was an underlying message of guilt by association, especially since the two major teachers' "unions" were the AFT and the NEA, which were also active in higher education. In the 1990s, public attitudes toward faculty unions in higher education remained lukewarm. During a strike by professors at the University of Cincinnati in 1993, for example, an editorial in the *Cincinnati Enquirer* expressed what was probably a widespread view: "Few will shed a tear for the most protected class of public employees, unionized university professors."[26]

In another development, governors and state legislators took a new interest in public higher education in the 1990s. One theme that emerged was the idea that public colleges and universities needed to markedly improve undergraduate education. This implied changes in faculty working arrangements. There was a renewed emphasis from state political leaders on classroom teaching; faculty research was viewed with increasing skepticism.[27]

Posing an even more direct challenge to faculty working arrangements were newfound interests of state politicians in the assessment and evaluation of faculty work. This turn of events, in tandem with stronger suggestions that colleges and universities should adopt more cost-effective practices from the business world, increased tensions among the faculties at many public institutions.[28] As the boards of some public institutions began to issue statements and policies that increasingly appeared to be rooted in conservative political ideology, the situation sometimes grew acrimonious.

Perhaps the most well-known case of a faculty organizing effort in the 1990s was as the University of Minnesota. Although that faculty eventually rejected collective bargaining, the fact that the faculty of a respected, research-oriented university had seriously considered unionization helped revive interest in faculty unions and collective bargaining.

In 1996, the University of Minnesota's board of regents announced that it would revisit and perhaps substantially alter the tenure policies of the institution.[29] Not surprisingly, the faculty strongly objected to this development. In response, an effort to unionize the various campuses of the university began. A drive to collect signatures from at least 30 percent of the faculty on the various campuses was soon under way. The process moved along quickly, and the required signatures were gathered at the Twin Cities, Morris, and Crookston campuses.[30]

Republican Governor Arne H. Carlson was drawn into the dispute and responded with a proposal to create a three-person panel to mediate the conflict.[31] In the meantime, the regents were unable to proceed with actions on the tenure policy while the organizing campaign was under way. Several weeks later, however, when organizers at the university's law school were unsuccessful in gathering sufficient signatures to authorize a collective bargaining election, the regents promptly instituted a revised tenure policy that only applied to the law school. This development heightened anger among members of the faculty across the campuses of the university and further escalated what had already become a very public row. Later, the regents greatly modified their original proposals, and the immediate threat to tenure seemed to have passed. The faculty voted against unionizing, and the episode was concluded.

There were also unionization efforts in other states during the 1990s, with mixed results. The faculty at institutions such as New Mexico Highlands University joined the ranks of unionized professors,[32] while the faculty at institutions such as Northern Illinois University rejected collective bargaining.[33] On balance, however, although the subject of faculty unions was discussed with more frequency, the movement made only modest gains throughout most of the 1990s.

The climate regarding unionization in the professions changed, at least to a small degree, by the close of the decade. With the enormous changes caused by the rise of managed care in the health care field, even the stalwart American Medical Association endorsed collective bargaining for physicians in 1999. For faculty unions in colleges and universities, the decade came to an end with hints that changes could come from the National Labor Relations Board. There was an increase in the number of NLRB members who were appointed by the Clinton administration, and in 1998, the NLRB determined that members of the faculty at the University of the Great Falls in Minnesota did not hold managerial positions and were therefore eligible for collective bargaining.[34] A similar finding was issued by a NLRB official in the case of Manhattan College in 1999, though that was appealed to the full board, and its fate remained uncertain at the end of the decade.

Whatever changes would come, however, the record through 1999 was clear. The *Yeshiva* decision was the primary, though not the only, force in quelling what had been a vigorous movement. After *Yeshiva*, there were few successful organizing attempts, and bargaining units were lost or challenged at dozens of institutions.[35]

CONCLUSION

As this brief overview suggests, the first decade of faculty unionization had a transformative effect on the higher education landscape. For a time, it seemed that rapid growth would continue indefinitely. What an overview such as this misses, of course, are the circumstances and nuances involved in the choice—and it is a choice—by a faculty to adopt collective bargaining.

To understand the dynamics of unionization more closely, the following chapters examine how the faculties of the Universities of Rhode Island, Massachusetts, and Connecticut came to choose collective bargaining. In many respects, the stories are organizational sagas and the emphasis is on organizational units and entities rather than individuals. These are also political sagas, at both macro- and micro-levels.

NOTES

1. See Everett Carll Ladd, Jr., and Seymour Martin Lipsett, *Professors, Unions, and American Higher Education* (Washington, DC: American Enterprise Institute, 1973), 6.

2. See Donald J. Keck, *The NEA and Academe Through the Years: The Higher Education Roots of NEA, 1857-Present* (Washington, DC: National Education Association, 1999).

3. Ibid.

4. Quoted in Clyde W. Barrow, *Universities and the Capitalist State: Corporate Liberalism and the Reconstruction of American Higher Education, 1894–1928* (Madison: University of Wisconsin Press, 1990), 183.

5. Johnstone, 6.

6. Ibid., 4.

7. Ibid.

8. Ibid.

9. U.S. Department of Labor, Bureau of Labor Statistics, *Handbook of Labor Statistics* (Washington, DC: U.S. Department of Labor, 1989), 475.

10. Joseph W. Garbarino and Bill Aussieker, *Faculty Bargaining: Change and Conflict* (New York: McGraw-Hill, 1975), 56.

11. Ibid.

12. Johnstone, pp. xiv–xv.

13. Burton R. Clark, *The Academic Life: Small Worlds, Different Worlds* (Princeton: The Carnegie Foundation for the Advancement of Teaching, 1987).

14. See Ladd and Lipsett.

15. Ibid, p. 17.

16. See Gordon B. Arnold and Ted I. K. Youn, "Evolving Public Discourse of Tenure and Academic Freedom, 1950s–1990s: A Frame Analysis." Paper presented at the Annual Meeting of the Assocation for the Study of Higher Education, Miami, November 1998.

17. Gene I. Maeroff, "College Faculties Are Building Union Muscle," *New York Times*, 4 June 1976.

18. *National Labor Relations Board v. Yeshiva University*, 444 U.S. 672 (1980), 103 LRRM, as quoted in Ernst Benjamin, "Faculty and Management Rights in Higher Education Collective Bargaining: A Faculty Perspective." Paper presented at the Annual Meeting of the Center for the Study of Collective Bargaining in Higher Education and the Professions, New York, 14 April 1997.

19. Ibid.

20. See Barbara A. Lee and James P. Begin, "Criteria for Evaluating the Managerial Status of College Faculty: Applications of *Yeshiva University* by the NLRB," *Journal of College and University Law* 10:4 (Spring 1984): 515–39.

21. "Yeshiva-watch: Year Six," *National Center for the Study of Collective Bargaining in Higher Education and the Professions Newsletter* 13:5 (November–December 1985).

22. See David Vogel, *Fluctuating Fortunes: The Political Power of Business in America* (New York: The Free Press, 1989).

23. See, for example, Will Miller, "Unionizing at the University of Vermont," *Thought and Action* 6:1 (Spring 1990).

24. "New Hampshire Faculty Votes to Unionize," *Chronicle of Higher Education*, 31 October 1990.

25. Courtney Leatherman, "Faculty Unions Lower Their Expectations in the Recession," *Chronicle of Higher Education*, 3 February 1993.

26. Quoted in Carolyn J. Mooney, "700 Professors Join Strike at University of Cincinnati," *Chronicle of Higher Education*, 7 April 1993.

27. Patricia Gumport, "Public Universities as Academic Workplaces," *Daedalus*, 126:4 (Fall 1997): 127.

28. Ibid.

29. These events were recounted in Denise K. Magner, "Minnesota Regents Change Tenure Policy for Their Law School," *Chronicle of Higher Education*, 15 November 1996.

30. The faculty of the Duluth campus of the University of Minnesota had been organized previously.

31. "Governor Enters Fray Over Tenure at U. [*sic*] of Minnesota," *Chronicle of Higher Education*, 11 October 1996.

32. Karla Haworth, "New Mexico Highlands University Faculty Votes to Unionize," *Chronicle of Higher Education*, 1 May 1998.

33. "Faculty Union Organizers Again fail to Win Over Professors," *Chronicle of Higher Education*, 19 May 1993.

34. Courtney Leatherman, "NLRB May End Its Opposition to Unions for Private Colleges," *Chronicle of Higher Education*, 9 January 1998.

35. Courtney Leatherman, "Union Movement at Private Colleges Awakens After 20-Year Slumber," *Chronicle of Higher Education*, 21 January 2000.

CHAPTER 4

Faculty Unionization at the University of Rhode Island

Of flagship public universities in southern New England, the faculty of the University of Rhode Island (URI) was the first to embrace unionism. It came amid a climate of economic crisis in the state and during a time of general upheaval at the university. Occurring during a period when antiwar protests involving students, and sometimes faculty, disrupted university life at times, the emergence of a faculty union was but one of many challenges that the campus faced. In the early 1970s, instability at the university was increasingly obvious throughout the state. A cluster of events with negative overtones kept the university in the spotlight. The actions and events at this, the only public university in the state, were treated as local news, sometimes eliciting spirited reaction from state politicians and the media.

Despite its rural and serene setting in Kingston and the pastoral aura of the nearby farmlands, the University of Rhode Island has been deeply connected to state life. Beginning its life as the State Agricultural School in 1888, it underwent several transformations, becoming the Rhode Island College of Agriculture and Mechanical Arts in 1892, then Rhode Island State College in 1909, and finally the University of Rhode Island in 1951. Less than an hour's drive from the state capital and urban center of Providence, little that transpires on campus escapes public notice. By the late 1960s, there were ample circumstances to attract attention. Within a few years, the university had amassed an enormous deficit. In the same period, state politicians grappled with the question of how public higher education should be structured, the upshot of which was a succession of three different governing boards assuming authority for the university in the span of only a few years. Added to this, the state legislature often took an activist role in dealing with the university, often complicating life for the university's administration.

In this milieu, Werner A. Baum assumed the presidency of the University of Rhode Island in 1968. New university presidents could not have expected a trouble-free tenure at that period in U.S. history. There were probably few, however, who foresaw the degree to which international and domestic events would soon challenge longstanding understandings and traditions on campuses across the nation. The war in Southeast Asia was a source of dissension, but no one could have anticipated the strong and widespread reactions to the secret bombing in Cambodia and to the deaths of four students at Kent State. Even less likely to be predicted was the magnitude of the downturn that would jolt the U.S. economy in the next decade. Nonetheless, those were the cards that were dealt to academic leaders in this period and, whether they liked it or not, these leaders soon discovered that little of past tradition could be taken for granted.

It is difficult not to harbor some sympathy for academic leaders who labored to carry on with the day-to-day business of managing campuses. Though, in the end, campus structures and processes proved remarkably resilient and largely escaped unscathed from the tribulations of the period, the uncertainty of the era made it difficult to attend to academic matters without encountering new complications. As the sands shifted beneath them, it was often difficult to anticipate how events would unfold or how they would be interpreted.

Many of these developments were still in the future at the beginning of Werner Baum's tenure. Yet, already in 1968, the signs of change were evident in Kingston. Although Baum would see much more upheaval before his departure five years later, a brief review of campus controversies during 1968 is helpful in understanding the context in which faculty unionism would come to URI.

One such event occurred when the Thiebault Commission, which had been promulgated by state political leaders, issued a report with recommendations for public higher education in the state. The political controversy that the report created within the URI faculty would prove to be one catalyst in the rise of unionism among the professors. In essence, the Thiebault Commission made recommendations that would completely restructure the long-standing governance arrangements for the state's public institutions of higher education.

Uneasy about what they saw as their minimal role in the Thiebault Commission's recommendations and about the direction in which the proposal would lead, members of the URI faculty responded with concern and established a special committee of their own. This faculty group, working under the auspices of the URI faculty senate, was charged with studying the Thiebault Commission's report and responding to it. In its report, the special committee of the faculty made clear its opposition to and alarm with the changes proposed by the Thiebault Commission. Characterizing the proposed changes as "regressive," the report of the faculty special committee further stated that:

The recommended subordination of higher education would seriously undermine the necessary participatory role of the governing board, the administration, the faculty, the students and the alumni in determining the nature and direction of higher education in the state.[1]

The faculty group was particularly concerned that the proposed new governance structure would lead to an increased level of partisan politics in university affairs. This, it was felt, would be a marked change from past practice. It had been widely agreed that the framers of the original 1939 legislation that had set up the existing structure had largely been successful in keeping this type of partisanship at minimal levels.[2]

Faculty displeasure with the Thiebault Commission's proposal had little effect, however. Much of the commission's report was incorporated in the Rhode Island Higher Education Act, enacted the following year. That legislation abolished the Board of Trustees of State Colleges, which had overseen university affairs for three decades. In its place, the legislation established a new nine-member Board of Regents effective July 1970.[3] (The nine-member Board would have a short run; it was abolished and replaced with a fifteen-member Board only three years later.)

Another source of tension at the university came in the aftermath of a million-dollar deficit that Baum had inherited. Although URI managed to nearly eliminate the deficit over a three- year span, by then the finances of the university had become closely watched by both the public and state political leaders. This attention had only intensified as a result of a scandal involving an attempt by a URI business office employee to embezzle university funds, which had occurred shortly before Baum's arrival. Indeed, the university budget and budgeting process were difficult issues throughout Baum's presidency, largely due to the pall that had been cast by the unfortunate events in the months before his incumbency.[4]

Sometimes smaller-scale issues sparked controversy. Although the events in Vietnam caused much protest on college and university campuses across the United States, including URI, students questioned the authority of campus leaders on a wide range of issues, often of purely local interest. In late 1968, the mundane matter of the academic calendar was the source of one such challenge at URI. The published academic calendar called for students to return to campus immediately after the New Year in order to attend final classes of the fall semester. This would be followed by final examinations about a week later. Upset that they would be required to return to campus on January 2 and 3, students mobilized for action. About 1,000 students attended a special meeting of the student senate on the topic and 4,000 signatures were gathered on a petition to cancel classes for the two days.[5]

The faculty senate soon addressed the problem. Convening on December 10 to resolve the matter, the faculty senate took the unusual step of allowing student protesters to attend the meeting. In the end, the faculty senate amended the calendar largely according to student wishes. The two days of classes were canceled and replaced by one additional class day on January 13, just prior to final examinations. This seemingly trivial episode illustrates the challenges to old assumptions about decision making and the distribution of power on the URI campus.[6] In the following year a student strike would not be averted, adding further to general unrest on campus.[7]

FACULTY SALARY ISSUE

Against this backdrop of uneasiness on campus, the matter of faculty salaries emerged. It was a controversy that would become instrumental in galvanizing sufficient support for faculty unionization. More than other faculty matters, the salary issue was played out on a public stage, and on that stage there was no doubt about the faculty's unhappiness. Far from being an issue confined to rumblings on campus, faculty discontent became front-page news in the state's major daily newspaper, the influential *Providence Journal*. Even Werner Baum was quoted as stating that the faculty was "understandably very, very disturbed."[8]

In comments to joint sessions of the Rhode Island House and Senate Finance Committees in March of 1969, Baum cited the faculty pay issue as "the single roughest issue" of his presidency to date. Although Baum was able to lift a freeze on the hiring of new faculty and assistants at about the same time, the fiscal situation remained precarious. Commenting on what he thought would be possible given the planned state budget allocation, he saw only "a minimal [sic] acceptable situation . . . I don't know how long we can keep riding this horse without real difficulty in retaining personnel."[9] The Rhode Island Education Association, the state affiliate of the NEA, echoed Baum's concern about low faculty salaries at URI and called on the governor and the state legislature to correct the situation.[10]

By year's end, however, little had changed. The faculty at URI, along with their colleagues at the other state institutions (Rhode Island College and Rhode Island Junior College), remained very unhappy with reported salary proposals for the 1970–71 academic year. They relayed this dissatisfaction to the board of trustees. Another source of unhappiness among the faculty was the process by which salary proposals were developed—a process that essentially excluded faculty. In a prophetic statement to the trustees, faculty representative Niels Rorholm stated that the lack of faculty voice in the budget process was helping to strengthen support for the idea of a faculty union among some of the faculty.[11]

Although the trustees planned to request a 13.4 percent increase for URI faculty (somewhat more than the requests for the other two state institutions), faculty representatives viewed this as inadequate and requested reconsideration. The trustees were reluctant to amend their planned request, because, as the chairwoman of the trustees asserted, "The state is in a serious fiscal situation. There is no guarantee we can even get what we requested."[12]

During this time, the *Providence Journal* reported on faculty issues at URI with regularity, bringing these matters into the public arena in a way that may not have been anticipated at the time. For example, President Baum's address to a local Rotary Club, an otherwise unremarkable event, received front-page treatment in the paper in an article with the headline, "URI Deficient in Two Areas, Baum Asserts."[13] (The two areas noted were the library and, again, faculty salaries.) Baum made the argument that in order to understand the URI faculty issue, it was necessary to compare the faculty salary situation at URI with those at comparable institutions. By comparing faculty salaries at URI with salaries at similar schools with good reputations, he believed, one would be able to judge whether or not faculty complaints about salary levels were or were not justified.

The question, of course, soon centered on which other institutions should comprise the comparison group. How favorably URI compared with other schools on the salary issue, of course, might vary greatly depending on which universities or colleges were included in the comparison group. It was Baum's opinion that URI should be included in a peer group that included the neighboring Universities of Massachusetts and Connecticut. (Average faculty salaries at both of these institutions were greater than at URI.) Such institutions, he noted, were within close relative geographic proximity to URI, and both shared a similar spirit and mission to URI's. Based on his own examination of URI faculty salaries, however, Baum had concluded that in terms of faculty salaries, URI was in the company of a different set of institutions. Faculty salaries at URI were more in keeping with those at institutions such as the University of Alabama at Birmingham, the University of West Florida, and Western Connecticut State College than at the flagship public campuses of Rhode Island's neighboring states.[14]

Again underscoring the increased public attention to URI matters, an editorial titled "URI's Weaknesses" appeared in the

Providence Journal five days later.[15] "There can be no quarreling with President Werner Baum's analysis of the University of Rhode Island's weaknesses," the editorial stated, adding that

On salaries, it may be that there is a bit more latitude for argument. Good teachers are not always the highest paid ones. . . . But in an age . . . when the "pirating" of faculty members is one of the hazards of a college president's life, there is a high correlation between the salary level and the quality of the faculty. . . . It is natural to compare conditions there [URI] with the nearest state universities in Connecticut and Massachusetts.[16]

As public debate about faculty salaries raged, the general finances of the university remained in question. In the temporary absence of Werner Baum (who was recuperating from surgery in January 1970), James E. Archer, vice president for academic affairs and the acting chief of URI, announced a meeting with the faculty to discuss the fiscal problems. This meeting, which was held on February 4, 1970, prompted yet another *Providence Journal* editorial. On this occasion, the *Journal* took a harder line than before on the issue of faculty pay increases. Stating that faculty salaries had become "a bleak issue on campus," the *Journal* stated that

the issue requires hard-headed negotiating, as is the case with any group of state employees, and therefore the meeting this week does resemble a negotiating session with the faculty members explaining more to the General Assembly than to URI officials their plea for higher pay.[17]

Thus, as the internal situation at URI grew more strained, a public awareness of faculty issues was formed in which the URI faculty was increasingly presented as simply another category of state employees. The logic that this rhetorical construction of the situation implied was that the faculty pay issue at URI could be resolved using the same mechanisms brought to bear in the state's dealings with other public employees.

As the events unfolded, then, it became evident that under the existing arrangements the administration and, perhaps, to some extent the university's governing board, were caught in a controversy that was largely between the faculty and the General Assembly. In a sense, the officials charged with overseeing URI seemed in increasing danger of becoming irrelevant onlookers in one of the major issues confronting the university.

At the February 4 meeting, it was confirmed that the university faced a new deficit, amounting to near $1 million. Though the proposed solution to the immediate problem that this created called for increased university fees and adjustments to the existing budget, many faculty members were generally understanding and showed at least some sympathy for the administration's situation. In fact, the faculty senate passed a resolution to this effect, commending the administration for the "forthright manner in which it presented to the university-at-large the matter of the existing budget deficit."[18]

By late spring, the Board of Trustees of State Colleges reached the conclusion that faculty salaries at URI, as well as the other public institutions, should be significantly increased. Having revisited the salaries in light of comparisons with the different sets of peer institutions that had been suggested some months earlier, the board had come to the view that increases would be necessary in order to make URI comparable to those institutions. This should have been good news for URI faculty who had been waiting for such a decision, but it turned out to have little effect.

Although the board of trustees had now taken a position substantially closer to that of the faculty, by May of 1970 the board was reluctant to take any action on its conclusions. The higher education reforms proposed by the legislature the previous year were about to go into effect, and the new board of regents, which was about to assume control of public higher education in Rhode Island, had announced its intention to abolish the board of trustees. Apparently not wanting to complicate matters by embarking on major decisions prior to the transition, the board opted to take no action in support of its conclusion that faculty salaries should be raised.[19]

THE ADVENT OF UNIONISM

It was upon this stage that faculty unionism grew. There was sufficient discontent within the faculty that in early 1970 there were public expressions of the view that collective bargaining should be investigated by the URI faculty. An ad hoc committee was formed in February 1970 to study this possibility. Though it is difficult to judge with authority, from their own perspective, members of the committee reported that they began their inquiry "undecided" about collective bargaining for the URI faculty and therefore without a predetermined view on that issue.[20]

They first addressed the matter of determining whether or not there was a legal basis for faculty to organize. On this, the 1966 legislation was clear. The committee was therefore able to confirm that "under the laws of Rhode Island, as amended, Chapter 36-11 of the State laws, entitled, 'Organization of State Employees," and Section 28-7-45 of the State Laws in 28-7, entitled, 'Labor Relations Act,' that the faculty is permitted to enter into collective bargaining."[21]

In gathering information, members of the committee also examined the faculty collective bargaining experience at other institutions. One member, for example, journeyed to the City University of New York to attend the National Conference on Collective Negotiations in Higher Education. Another member traveled to Rutgers to interview members of the faculty and administration at that university about the nature of their experience with collective bargaining.[22]

Events during the summer of 1970, which at first seemed unrelated, did nothing to reduce anxiety among the faculty. A course titled "Revolution in the Modern World" was slated as a summer offering by the university. Prior to the summer term, Baum's office received at least one complaint about the course. Pressured to do something because of the course's allegedly controversial and radical perspectives, Baum abruptly canceled it. This obviously pleased critics, but set off alarms about academic freedom on campus. Baum quickly reconsidered his decision, and only six days later the course was resurrected, apparently after the instructor gave sufficient assurances that the course would not be a one-sided polemic. Unfortunately, this chain of events left the general public with the idea that URI had a president incapable to standing up to radical elements within the faculty.[23] At the same time, vague and amorphous fears about limitations to academic freedom among faculty now seemed to have a concrete basis.

It is difficult to gauge how much influence the summer events had on faculty attitudes about collective bargaining, but it cannot have helped matters, especially since the salary issues had not abated. Several months later, the ad hoc faculty committee issued a report. The recommendation was that the URI faculty should adopt collective bargaining. This news reached the pages of the *Providence Journal*, although it treated the story as a pedestrian affair. The writers for the paper had concluded, "The tone of the report of the special committee to the faculty senate was one of cooperation with the administration." The fact that the faculty had little direct quarrel with President Baum, who had been generally supportive of faculty calls for higher salaries, did not mean that all was well, however. The chair of the special committee, Agnes Doody, had been quite clear that there was an active dispute. The controversy was not with Baum, however, but rather with the governing board.[24]

The situation only worsened when the regents subsequently voted to reduce their budget proposal for the following academic year. This new governing board—which was thought by some to be a new source of patronage—faced a skeptical faculty audience in budgetary decisions.[25] An uproar was created in the wake of that decision, which called for 7 percent faculty salary increases— a significant reduction from the previously discussed 12 percent. Five members of the Compensation Committee summarily issued their resignations from that body, capturing the attention of the *Providence Journal*, which gave front-page treatment to what was clearly seen as a dramatic escalation of tensions on campus. According to the *Journal*'s account, "The mass action to demonstrate growing dissatisfaction with the existing salary procedures was being interpreted last night as an indication that the URI faculty is moving closer to formal collective bargaining on salaries."[26]

The co-chairs of the Compensation Committee, L. Patrick Devlin and Leila Cain, had submitted a joint letter of resignation, excerpts of which were published in the *Providence Journal* account. Devlin and Cain stated that "for too long the faculty has had to subsidize higher education whenever budget cuts were necessitated by Rhode Island's continued financial difficulties. . . . The committee has lived with a number of governors, boards, presidents and budget crises. The facts change but the problem remains. URI faculty salaries are well below what they should be." They added that

The faculty of the University . . . is underpaid. The faculty Senate designated its Compensation Committee as the faculty's representative in matters of compensation. Yet while this committee has functioned, the gap between U.R.I.'s salaries and those four comparison institutions has widened. . . . [Given this situation] nothing this Committee recommends has a realistic chance of being implemented.[27]

As a consequence, Professors Devlin and Cain reported that they had resolved to "do all in our power to see that the faculty does have an effective voice in matters of compensation through equitable procedures such as collective bargaining."[28]

Although the Compensation Committee had failed to reach its goals, the ad hoc committee did not believe that this outcome was the "fault" of the URI administration. Again, they traced the problem back to the Board of Regents and its commissioner. The ad hoc committee reported its distress that "after nine years of trying to *catch up* [sic] to the *average* [sic] (an odious concept) we are still not at the mid-way point." [29] The committee therefore endorsed the mechanism of collective bargaining, which it regarded as "a more effective means of closing the salary gap" and one that could "prohibit the kinds of unilateral decision-making concerning faculty salaries that were made by [the] Commissioner . . . to the Board of Regents."[30]

In promoting the idea of collective bargaining, the committee also considered the implications that this course would have for the university's faculty senate. On this question, they saw collective bargaining and the faculty senate as "dual instruments of the general faculty." Having investigated the question in detail, then, the committee formally recommended to the senate that the faculty of the University of Rhode Island enter into collective bargaining with the Board of Regents.[31]

The faculty senate took up the matter on February 11, 1971. With little acrimony, and with only one vote short of a unanimous decision, the senate gave its endorsement to collective bargaining.[32] Perhaps less surprising than the final vote itself was the ease with which it was made. As *Providence Journal* writer Carol J. Wright reported, "The absence of any fiery debate over a recommendation that a 'community of scholars' [quotation marks in original] turn to unionism and the subsequent nearly unanimous voice vote surprised some senate members and onlookers."[33] With the faculty senate committed to this course, the next step was to bring the matter to the entire faculty. As these developments seemed to indicate that momentum toward a faculty union was building, all of the players inched closer to the point where state labor laws would dictate the procedures and flow of events. Once sufficient cards endorsing a collective bargaining election were signed and collected (in this case about 180 of the 600 faculty members), the actions of faculty union advocates and opponents, of administrators and board members in the decision-making process would be severely prescribed. The norms and rules of higher education would now take a secondary role to Rhode Island's labor laws and regulations governing public sector employment.

The unionization issue was debated at a meeting of about 150 faculty members that was organized by the faculty senate in early March.[34] One subject of debate was the effect that a faculty union and collective bargaining would have on the relationship between the faculty and the Board of Regents. Yet, when one faculty member in attendance suggested that unionization would bring about an "adversary relationship," the response from unionization supporters was that this adversarial situation already prevailed.[35] The problem, in the eyes of union supporters, was that the Regents were too closely allied with the interests of the legislature.[36]

A newsletter issued in April 1971 by the Rhode Island Education Association (RIEA-NEA), the state NEA affiliate articulated three major reasons for the rise of unionism at URI. First, it was contended that an "equitable voice" for the faculty could only come through collective bargaining. Second was the claim that faculty senates (including, apparently, their own) were "impotent" structures that were ineffective at dealing with faculty matters. Finally, it was stated that only collective bargaining could stave off budget cuts in light of the bleak economic situation of the university at the time.[37]

The committee on collective bargaining had also investigated the matter of what organization might become the bargaining agent in a collective bargaining situation. They researched the AAUP, the AFT, and the Rhode Island Education Association, the last being the NEA's local affiliate. The AFT had already been active in Rhode Island's public institutions of higher education. The chapter at Rhode Island College (the state's sole public four-year college) had already made two unsuccessful attempts, in 1968 and 1969, to organize the faculty at that institution.[38] After some investigation, however, the committee came to the view that the best choice would be either to choose RIEA-NEA or else to develop a freestanding group with no outside affiliation at all.[39]

The AFT never emerged as a major player in the URI campaign, but the local AAUP chapter continued its efforts. The AAUP held an open meeting to present its point of view to the faculty at large on March 9, 1971. Albert J. Hoban of the administration met with both Dean Batrouka of the campus AAUP chapter and Pat Devlin of the local NEA-National Society of Professors on April 8 in order to "set up ground rules so that the university could maintain its position of neutrality on the question of which organization, if any, the faculty or other members of the university desire to represent them."[40] After that meeting, President Baum sent a memorandum to the entire faculty seeking to assure them of the university's "strict neutrality" in the organizing drive.[41]

Patricia Houlihan, president of the Rhode Island Federation of Teachers–AFT, sent a letter to all URI faculty in April urging them to sign cards and, of course, asking for the designation of that organization as the bargaining agent.[42] In its monthly newsletters, URIPA (the University of Rhode Island Professional Association, affiliate of the Rhode Island Education Association) was similarly requesting support for the unionization cause and itself as the preferred bargaining agent.[43]

With the unionization drive gaining momentum, the URI chapters of the AAUP and of the URIPA both voted to pursue the right to represent the faculty as its bargaining agent.[44] Rhode Island labor law dictated that to bring the matter to an election, 30 percent of the potential bargaining unit members would need to sign cards requesting an election. For a second group to contest the right to represent members of the bargaining unit, they would need to obtain cards from 15 percent of those who were eligible. This situation made it clear that although there was considerable doubt about what organization might be victorious in seeking to represent the faculty, both groups were confident that union support among the faculty was strong.

In the scramble to obtain signed cards, it took only two weeks for URIPA to gather them from over 30 percent of the faculty. Having met this requirement, it immediately filed for an election with the state.[45] With momentum on their side and time remaining in the semester winding down, URIPA leaders originally hoped to obtain an election date prior to the summer. There were still obstacles to overcome, however, and with the summer exodus from Kingston fast approaching, it became clear that time was running out for an election in the current academic year.

A major obstacle was encountered in the next step in the process. The executive director of the state labor relations board, Angelo E. Azzinaro, set a conference date in May for the petitioning group and the regents. At that meeting the order of business would be to address the matter of precisely defining who would and would not be included in the potential bargaining unit.[46] As events unfolded, it became clear that the matter of department chairs was a source of disagreement between the university and pro-union groups. At the State Board of Labor Relations hearing on May 24, 1971, the regents formally proposed the exclusion of department chairs and directors from any faculty bargaining unit.[47] Not unexpectedly, the parties failed to reach agreement about the issue, and another hearing was scheduled for June 14.

The question of department-chair eligibility was a relatively common one in faculty unionization efforts, but that did not make the issue any less thorny for those at URI. The university position was that chairpersons should be excluded from a faculty bargaining unit because the chairpersons were performing management functions. Along the same lines, the administration sent letters to faculty serving in various directors' positions informing those faculty of the university's view that each of these appointments was an administrative position.[48] Faculty organizers obviously disagreed with that position. Still, without a decision on these questions, the regents were successful in delaying any election until the fall.[49]

As the debate about bargaining-unit eligibility continued, members of the faculty were becoming increasingly alarmed at the general state of affairs at the university. This feeling was exacerbated when, in mid-June, four faculty members announced their intention to leave the university altogether. Among those making an exit was Frederick H. Fisher, chair of the physics department, who told the press that he had concluded that "the Rhode Island legislature does not regard education as a good investment in the future of the state."[50] In his view, the necessary funds to operate a competitive physics program had not been forthcoming in state appropriations, and prospects for improvement to the situation looked dim. In a letter to colleagues, excerpts of which were subsequently published in the *Providence Journal*, Fisher explained that the "conditions for the operation of the department had changed drastically" since his arrival on campus, especially with regard to space and funding. He also stated:

We need 5,000 square feet of space for research and instruction, and it has been refused for lack of funds. We have tremendous crowding in our elementary physics laboratories where there are four people working in space for two. We need space for research. I had received permission from the National Science Foundation to bring my own research here but I wasn't able to bring it for lack of facilities.[51]

The response to the resignations of Fisher and the other faculty members—two from the graduate program in speech pathology and audiology and one from industrial and ocean engineering—was one of alarm. Speaking of Fisher's imminent departure, a member of the physics department was quoted as stating, "We have never had anyone of his stature in this department. My reaction to the resignation is that this is the death blow to the hopes of the department for the foreseeable future."[52] Of another departure, the dean of the College of Engineering said, "The loss to Rhode Island of this man's talent, initiative and teaching ability is inestimable. Also lost is the money he would have attracted for teaching and research. . . . The stars are the ones that go."[53]

Even the URI president concurred in the negative assessment of the situation, noting that the resignation of prominent faculty members was a loss. Although Baum attempted to cast some positive light on the overall situation, he nonetheless commented that "in the short run I am pessimistic" and that "the tragedy [of URI's circumstance] is that you tend to lose your best people. . . . It takes years to attract top people, and you tend to lose them in a hurry."[54]

The *Providence Journal* account of the resignations made it clear
that faculty salary issues were also closely linked to the resignations. As reported in that publication, one of those who would be
departing (associate professor of industrial and ocean engineering Joseph Stanislao) was expected to receive a $7,000 salary in-
crease when he moved to Cleveland State University. Perhaps
more important than the wrangling over faculty salaries, however,
was the *Journal's* insistence that something was amiss at the university. Prominent faculty members—people acknowledged, even
by members of the administration, as "stars," and representative
of the university's highest aspirations—were leaving abruptly.
The implication was that the problem was not within the university itself, but in the political realm beyond it. Moreover, far from
rallying to the defense of the legislature or the regents, top university officials, up to and including the president, agreed with
the departing professors' bleak assessment of the situation. This
constituted further evidence of the widening rift between the faculty and state entities with influence over the university. It seems
unlikely that when state lawmakers originally enacted legislation
enabling public employee collective bargaining a few years earlier, they imagined that one result would be the unfolding state
of affairs with the university faculty.

With the election delayed, the situation remained unresolved.
In the fall there were public airings of the various positions as the
campaign continued. For example, a three-way debate was held
on October 28, featuring representatives of URIPA and the local
AAUP chapter—both groups supporting an affirmative vote for
collective bargaining—and representatives of the Faculty for Professional Freedom at URI, whose members opposed unionization.[55] Several days later, the University Debate Union sponsored
another program, which was billed as "Collective Bargaining; Yes
or No?" with L. Patrick Devlin taking the "yes" position and C.
Richard Skogley representing the "no" position.[56]

Within the administration, it was observed that the tenor of the
campaign was becoming increasingly tense. Commenting on the
general tone of the literature being circulated, one administrator
wrote of his concern that "The party is getting a little rough."[57]
The spirited debate—sometimes veering into acrimony—not only
engaged supporters and opponents of unionization, but often

raged between the two major groups supporting a faculty union. In their zeal to persuade the faculty that their respective organizations would be the best choice as a bargaining agent, there was a constant barrage of pamphleteering, memorandum writing, and lobbying. Few chances to one-up the other group were missed. When the NEA was successful in a union election in the Pennsylvania system, for example, its local affiliate, the URIPA, touted this outcome in an October newsletter, boasting that "NEA has never lost to the AAUP. We are confident that same fact will hold true at URI!"[58] AAUP representatives countered with a missive declaring "Vote AAUP! Achieve a truly *professional* [emphasis in original] contract!"[59]

Meanwhile, the new group called Faculty for Professional Freedom at URI was making the case against unionization. The group was a relative latecomer to the debate. In a letter to the faculty in November, the group stated that "it should be pointed out that in the past year the Univ. [*sic*] of Mass. [*sic*] at Amherst received 11% *without* [emphasis in original] collective bargaining but that SMU [Southeastern Massachusetts University] only had 5% with collective bargaining."[60] In a subsequent memorandum, the group argued to the faculty that "we are likely to lose more than we can possibly gain." The group further stated:

We do not believe that assuming a *labor* [*sic*] posture (vs. management) is appropriate for the faculty. . . . URIPA emphasizes coercion—bringing the force of numbers (largely outside the university) and large sums of money available from NEA, with the threat or actuality of strike to force concessions. AAUP is a reluctant contender . . . The local chapter of the AAUP (now estimated to number about 130 members) has in recent years not demonstrated capable management, and there is doubt that it has enjoyed the confidence of the URI faculty. . . . It did much good for the URI faculty in its formative years, but it does not appear now to be in a position to act effectively.[61]

In response to assertions made by the Faculty for Professional Freedom, URIPA stated that "URIPA has not responded to recent newsletters of the Faculty for Professional Freedom. . . . [T]heir facts are so grossly in error that we know most faculty will not be influenced by them. We are sure that FPF have made their errors unintentionally—they simply lack exact and *accurate* [emphasis in original] information about [collective] bargaining."[62]

To many in the faculty, it seemed that the unionization movement had momentum. Some of those who did not favor this outcome nonetheless began to see the need to think about their options in the event that faculty collective bargaining was brought to campus.

A group of faculty in the College of Business Administration, however, observed that a union did not seem to have much to offer them. They called on their colleagues to help devise a strategy to protect their interests, which, they believed, were substantially different from those of many members of the faculty in other URI colleges. The group was especially concerned about a leveling effect that unionization could have on salaries across the different schools and disciplines. They believed that they were deserving of higher salaries and that this outcome was not unfair, but simply a reflection of market forces. This line of thinking suggested that with other venues in which they could ply their trades—such as the various levels of government and the private sector—members of the business administration faculty rightfully commanded higher wages than did faculty members in other areas, particularly those with specialties in areas such as literature and other traditional arts and sciences fields.[63]

The situation had grown increasingly uncomfortable within the administration. Though officially neutral, the general line of argument emanating from the administration tended to stress the idea that a faculty union would result in a management-labor–type of antagonism between faculty (as workers) and the administration. Both union advocates and opponents seemed to reach a similar conclusion on this matter. Still, the president's office attempted to keep the situation on an even keel. In a letter circulated to all members of the faculty in November, President Baum took pains to assure them that the "only issue raised by the University before the State Labor Relations Board concerned the eligibility of department chairmen."[64] Yet Baum was clearly disillusioned by the prospect of a unionized faculty. Two weeks later, in a speech before the Conference of Southern Academic Deans, he stated that in his view university legislative bodies, rather than unions, were better ways to proceed. Still, it was his belief that "the trend toward unionism among faculty is a symptom, not the disease."[65]

Beyond the tense situation on campus, the dispute in the wider political realm continued. In a telegram to the Board of Regents, dated November 3, 1971 (and subsequently quoted in the URIPA Newsletter), Devlin charged that the regents were attempting to "lock up" the university budget prior to the union election, adding that URIPA expected to win the upcoming election and was formally (and publicly) proposing to meet with representatives of the regents over budget issues two days after the election.[66]

This tactic drew sharp criticism from the faculty senate. In fact, in a letter to Devlin, Stephen D. Schwarz, president of the faculty senate, wrote that the executive committee objected to Devlin's suggestions, particularly his invoking language about "locking up" the budget. In a reprimanding tone, Schwarz reminded Devlin that the senate and faculty would not be obligated by the comments in Devlin's original telegram.[67] It seems that the issue here was less about what was said than about Devlin's preemptive and implicit claim to speak for the faculty. Nonetheless, Schwarz's letter was soon made public by the executive committee, further bringing the internal squabbling to a wider audience.

The situation remained largely unchanged until the election in November. On December 1, 1971, the state labor relations board announced the outcome of the election. A total of 563 of 669 eligible faculty members had cast ballots. Of these, the pro-union vote was split between the University of Rhode Island Professional Association (121 votes) and the AAUP (161) votes. Although together this amounted to 282 votes (a slim, one-vote majority if taken together), the outcome also meant that 281 persons voted for no union at all. [68] However, the important point was that no one choice had received more than the required 50 percent result that would settle the matter. Under such circumstances, a runoff election between the top two choices was mandated.

At this point, the question was whether the AAUP could successfully capture the votes of those who had voted in this first election for URIPA. Additionally, the nonvoters in the first election represented another possible source of support for the runoff election. The outcome was not certain, but URIPA had stated that

"Collective bargaining by either the URIPA or the AAUP is better than no bargaining at all!"[69] It therefore lent its support to AAUP, rather than see the unionization bid defeated altogether.

Although the result of the second election was not a landslide, the union camp maintained its unified position. The tally in the runoff showed 293 votes for the AAUP and 289 for "no union." Although 3 votes were challenged, this would still have left the "no union" position one vote shy of a tie. It was a slim margin of victory, but a victory nonetheless. The choice for collective bargaining was declared, and AAUP was selected as the faculty agent.

NOTES

1. "Thiebault Proposal Scored by URI Unit," *Providence Journal*, 1 January 1969.
2. Ibid.
3. Kevin J. Logan, Introductory notes, 1985, Records of the President's Office, [introduction], Mss. University of Rhode Island, University Library, Archives and Special Collections (hereafter referred to as URIA), 4.
4. Logan, 6. URIA.
5. "URI Faculty Body Cancels Classes 1st Week in Jan," *Providence Journal*, 11 December 1968.
6. Ibid.
7. The memory of campus unrest the previous year was still a concern as the 1970–71 academic year began. Seeking answers about how deteriorating events had culminated in a student strike, an ad hoc committee of ten faculty members, three students, and one member of the administration was created in September. Though focused on that event, the committee also was charged with investigating general unrest on campus.
8. "URI Faculty Upset Over Low Salaries," *Providence Journal*, 21 March 1969.
9. Ibid.
10. "Education Groups Support Baum on Pay at URI," *Providence Journal*, 22 March 1969.
11. Carol J. Young, "Faculties Protest Pay Raise Proposals," *Providence Journal*, 11 November 1969.
12. Ibid.

13. Ronald P. Furie, "URI Deficient in Two Areas, Baum Asserts," *Providence Journal*, 25 November 1969.

14. Ibid.

15. "URI's Weaknesses," *Providence Journal*, 30 November 1969.

16. Ibid.

17. "Comparing Salaries," *Providence Journal*, 4 February 1970.

18. Quoted in "Faculty Lauds URI Chief for Airing Deficit," *Providence Journal*, 20 February 1970.

19. "Trustees Back Faculty Pay Hikes; Approve No Policy," *Providence Journal*, 8 May 1970.

20. Ad Hoc Committee to Study the Desirability of Collective Bargaining, "Final Report," n.d. URIA.

21. Ibid.

22. Ibid.

23. Logan, 2. URIA.

24. Ibid.

25. Logan, 6. URIA.

26. Carol J. Young, "Five to Quit URI's Salary Committee," *Providence Journal*, 2 February 1971.

27. Patrick Devlin and Leila S. Cain, Memorandum to Walter C. Mueller, 29 January 1971, URIA.

28. Ibid.

29. Ibid.

30. Ibid.

31. Ibid.

32. Carol J. Wright, "URI Faculty Senate for Bargaining Right," *Providence Journal*, 12 February 1971.

33. Ibid.

34. "URI Faculty Debates Unionism," *Providence Journal*, 3 March 1971.

35. Ibid.

36. Ibid.

37. URI Professional Association (NEA-RIEA), [newsletter]:1, April 1971, URIA.

38. Carol J. Young, "Faculty group at URI Asks Bargaining Vote," *Providence Journal*, 27 April 1971.

39. Ibid., p. 6

40. Albert J. Hoban, Memorandum to Werner Baum, 14 April 1971, URIA.

41. Werner Baum, Memorandum to faculty, 22 April 1971, URIA.

42. P. Houlihan, Letter to faculty, 2 April 1971, URIA.

43. *URIPA Newsletter*, 1:2, April 1971, URIA.

44. "Groups Vie to Represent URI Faculty," *Providence Journal* 1 April 1971.

45. *URIPA Newsletter*, 1:3, April 1971, URIA.

46. Ibid.

47. *URIPA Newsletter*, 1:6, May 1971, URIA.

48. Various letters from the Office of the President and Office of the Vice President, dated June 18, 1971.

49. *URIPA Newsletter*, 1:5, May 1971, URIA.

50. Frederick H. Fisher, quoted in Lee Dykas, "Threatened Cut at URI Brings 4 Resignations," *Providence Journal*, 20 June 1971.

51. Ibid.

52. Ibid.

53. Quoted in Ibid.

54. Ibid.

55. "Debate on Collective Bargaining, October 28, 1971," Undated announcement (ephemera), URIA.

56. Ibid.

57. Author not identified, Note to Werner Baum, 26 October 1971, URIA.

58. *UIRPA Newsletter*, 2:4, October 1971, URIA.

59. URI-AAUP, Memorandum, n.d. URIA.

60. Faculty for Professional Freedom at URI, Memorandum 17 November 1971, URIA.

61. Faculty for Professional Freedom at URI, November 1971, URIA.

62. *URIPA Newsletter*, 2:9, November 1971, URIA.

63. G. Booth, R. Poulsen, B. Sanderson, and E. Smith, Memorandum to College of Business Faculty, 4 October 1971, URIA.

64. Werner Baum, Letter to faculty, 17 November 1971, URIA.

65. Werner Baum, Address to Conference of Southern Academic Deans, 30 November 1971, 8. URIA.

66. *URIPA Newsletter*, 2:6, November 1971, URIA.

67. Stephen D. Schwarz, Letter to L. Devlin, 15 November 1971, URIA.

68. State of Rhode Island, Board of Labor Relations, 1 December 1971, URIA.

69. *URIPA Newsletter*, 2:9, November 1971, URIA.

CHAPTER 5

Failure and Success at the University of Massachusetts

The distance between Amherst and Boston is less than ninety miles, but politically it sometimes seems as if these communities were situated on different continents. The rural town of Amherst lies far from the political epicenter of Massachusetts government. Though in many respects the University of Massachusetts (UMass) has remained dependent on decisions and policies made in Boston, events at the state's flagship public university only rarely have attracted major attention from either political elites or the news media. As a result, members of the university community often have a sense that officials in Boston do not understand or appreciate either the needs of their institution or its importance to the Commonwealth.

In Boston there are numerous institutions of higher education, many with national and international reputations. Harvard, MIT, Boston University, Tufts, as well a host of other schools in or near the city, command public attention in a way that the flagship UMass campus in Amherst does not. As late as 1962, David Riesman and Christopher Jencks noted that the University of Massachusetts was "still commonly thought of as a hick school."[1] Undoubtedly, the concentration of higher education in the Boston area, and especially the presence of so many world-renowned institutions, has been partially responsible for the lesser amount of attention given to the public university at Amherst.

These circumstances played an important role in the unionization of the faculty at the University of Massachusetts. The eventual adoption of a faculty union at UMass was, in large measure, a function of the state political environment and of state budgetary woes that had reached a crisis point. These external forces played a significant part in creating a milieu in which the University of Massachusetts faculty would consider organizing a union for collective bargaining. To understand the circumstances that led to faculty unionization, it is first necessary to consider the evolution of the university.

In 1867, the state established the Massachusetts Agricultural College amid the farmlands of the mid-state town of Amherst. Six decades later, in 1931, the school had sufficiently broadened its scope to warrant a name change to Massachusetts State College. Throughout these years, there was little political will to establish a public university in Massachusetts. The State College and a few other public postsecondary institutions sufficed. It was not until the 1940s that support for the idea of establishing a public university in the Commonwealth gathered any momentum. Even then, there was still uncertainty about where a state university should be situated. Several proposals were floated in the state legislature, and various locales were suggested as the best site. Some influential groups, including leading labor organizations, favored locating a public university in or near the state's urban center of Boston, while others suggested simply transforming the State College in Amherst. After several false starts, the legislature approved the Amherst option. This outcome represented an important victory for political leaders of that area, who fought vigorously for this result.[2] The selection of a site so far removed from the center of state politics had both positive and negative implications, however. Amherst did offer the possibility of building a new institution away from the constant gaze of state political elites, but its remoteness also held the potential for mutual misunderstanding. And such misunderstandings soon began to surface.

Although a board of trustees was established to oversee the new university (the other state higher education institutions were not under its auspices), the legislature retained much authority for itself. These were critical years in American higher education, and the university had been established near the beginning of the enormous expansion of higher education that followed the Second

World War. Within a few years, the lack of autonomy came to be viewed as a significant hindrance to the university's development. By the early 1960s, there were increasing complaints about the situation.

In response, a Special Commission on Budgetary Powers of the University of Massachusetts was formed in 1962, which was charged with examining conflicts between the state and the university regarding control of the university purse strings. In subsequent legislation, the board of trustees was granted more authority over the affairs of the university, particularly in the areas of personnel management, fiscal control, purchasing, printing, and staff travel. Still, in several important areas the legislature retained control. It maintained authority over appropriations—meaning that budget requests had to follow state regulations—and continued a policy of mandatory management and financial reports that were subject to review by the state auditor. As signed into law by Governor John A. Volpe, these changes did give additional autonomy to the university. Yet, the substantial authority that resided with the legislature tempered these advances. And, overall the university's fiscal situation remained closely linked to that of the state.[3]

These developments were not surprising given the traditions of Massachusetts state politics. It was business as usual in the Commonwealth to find a state entity with complicated patterns of authority. The state was well known for its high level of decentralization and its often-confusing system of boards and commissions.[4] The original intent of this approach was to place boards and commissions beyond the reach of political meddling. Results were mixed, however, and it was not unusual to find boards taking actions that contradicted the policy intentions of the governor, the legislature, or both.[5] Further complicating this arrangment, the terms of appointment for many board and commission members did not coincide with the term of the governor appointing them. As a result, prior to leaving office a governor sometimes had the opportunity to appoint numerous board members whose terms would extend beyond the governor's term in office. This increased the likelihood that an incoming governor would be forced to contend with a board or commission stacked with members who held views contrary to those of the new governor.[6] Under these circumstances, it was sometimes difficult to exert control over boards and commissions. It was not surprising, therefore, that the legislature was reluctant to grant to the board of trustees a broader degree of authority for the university than it did. This complicated interplay of interests among the board, the governor, and the legislature would have important implications in the heated political battle over faculty unionization at UMass in the following decade. In the early 1960s, however, these were simply political realities.

By the early 1970s, several circumstances had developed that set the stage for unionism among the UMass faculty in Amherst. Following the federal example, state legislation was enacted that permitted public employees in Massachusetts to unionize for collective bargaining. Many of these employees exercised this new right, especially in the teaching and public safety professions. Though public employees in Massachusetts were forbidden to bargain over wages and could not strike, the emergence of unions and collective bargaining among public sector employees was a major development. Groups such as the Massachusetts Federation of Teachers and the Massachusetts Teachers Association (MTA)— the state affiliate of the National Education Association—became powerful voices in the State House.[7]

At this same time, the state economy took a turn for the worse. During the incumbency of Republican Governor Francis Sargent the state's fiscal plight became increasingly serious.[8] This placed a substantial strain on all levels of state government, which were asked to make significant reductions in spending. In many quarters—public higher education among them—officials had grown unaccustomed to budgeting in conditions of scarcity, and these requests for cuts were unwelcome developments. So the emerging fiscal crisis—which, by the middle of the decade would result in a budget deficit of half a billion dollars—was escalating at the same moment that the state's public workers were beginning to recognize the value of collective action.

Although budget cuts were widely requested from state agencies and offices, the University of Massachusetts had a strong financial advocate in Robert C. Wood, its president. Wood, who came to the university in 1970, was well known and respected in academic circles for his work on urban politics and had served a stint in Washington at the Department of Housing and Urban Development. He was a shrewd politician and demonstrated skillful mastery of the intricacies of Massachusetts state politics. He soon proved to be a formidable advocate for the university. The university's budget request, submitted in September 1972, for example, would have set a new record if approved. Governor Sargent was displeased with this action, which was clearly out of line with his wishes for a more modest proposal. The governor did not hide his disapproval and stated in the press that he gave the university's request a "thumbs down."[9] Still, as the budgeting process unfolded Wood was able to obtain much of what he requested from the legislature over Sargent's objections.

In reviewing the relationship between the state and the university in its first few decades, then, it is apparent that by the early 1970s, significant tensions had emerged. Although in previous years the university was viewed favorably by the Boston political establishment, the escalating budget crisis exposed the tenuous three-way relationship among the university, the legislature, and the governor's office. By this time, it was evident that if university leaders were to advance their vision for the institution, they would need to take an active role in political battles at the State House. If this meant working with legislative leaders to obtain outcomes that were counter to the governor's policies, UMass officials showed a willingness to do so.

The faculty of UMass was largely absent from this picture. The external relations between university and the state had attracted relatively little attention from the faculty during the period of rapid growth at the university. The administration had often been successful in obtaining enough support to improve the situation of the faculty during the period of expansion. As the faculty professionalized, it had slowly acquired more influence over the traditionally hierarchical institution. By the 1970s, however, circumstances were changing. In addition to the pressures exerted by state politics and the state economy, Robert Wood's presidency exhibited a tendency toward centralized control.

Wood's penchant for reserving much authority for his office often was at odds with faculty expectations that had slowly developed in the preceding years.[10] Against the backdrop of all these changes, the idea of a faculty union began to emerge.

THE FIRST CAMPAIGN

Background

The rise of pro-union sentiment at the University of Massachusetts was a complex process that unfolded in fits and starts. It took two campaigns before the UMass faculty would vote favorably on the adoption of a union and collective bargaining. An unsuccessful campaign for unionization was held in 1973. Seemingly a dead issue at that point, it was only three years later that the issue was put to a vote again. In the second attempt, union organizers were successful. A look at both campaigns reveals the deepseated tensions that eventually resulted in faculty unionization.

The 1973 campaign emerged from a situation that one account characterized as "the slowing down of growth on the Amherst campus, after a decade of rapid expansion. . . . Higher education . . . [was] no longer the fairhaired child of the public sector. The legislature [was] . . . calling for belt tightening in all departments."[11] As the University of Massachusetts had evolved from a rural state college into a large multiversity, one side effect was an increasing complexity in the relationship between the faculty and the administration. The state's fiscal difficulties—prompting freezes on compensation and wages in the early 1970s—exacerbated these circumstances. Viewing these deteriorating conditions with concern were two faculty organizations on campus—a local chapter of the AAUP that had been established in the 1950s and a group that would become a major player on campus, called the Massachusetts Society of Professors (MSP). The MSP was a new group affiliated with the Massachusetts Teachers Association, which itself was the state affiliate of the NEA).

As early as 1970, the AAUP chapter began to explore what the faculty thought about the idea of a union, and it had conducted a survey on the subject of faculty collective bargaining. At that time, support was ambivalent. Another survey the following year told a different story, showing a dramatic increase in support for collective bargaining among faculty members on campus (see Table 5.1).

One of the AAUP chapter's concerns was what it viewed as the faculty's limited role in campus decision making. A chapter news-

Table 5.1

Results of Faculty Survey Concerning the Adoption of Collective
Bargaining at the University of Massachusetts, Amherst

	Fall 1970	Fall 1971
In favor of faculty collective bargaining	39%	50%
Oppose faculty collective bargaining	34%	30%
Undecided	26%	20%
No answer	1%	—

Source: AAUP Newsletter, University of Massachusetts Chapter (1972), Volume 2,
no. 4, November, p. 2.

letter from late 1971, for example, commented that there was "not
yet a formal mechanism for faculty participation at the system
level, [and] it is becoming increasingly difficult to incorporate
faculty opinion into the decision-making process."[12] The outlook
for the resolution of ongoing faculty salary issues continued to
look bleak, and in January 1972 the AAUP chapter announced that
it would adopt the new strategy of the national office and would
pursue collective bargaining.[13]

Although the UMass faculty senate had been working on faculty issues, the AAUP chapter leadership was frustrated with
what it saw as the board of trustees' consistent rebuffs of faculty
senate proposals. Though the AAUP group saw a role for the senate in the future, it thought that the senate's effectiveness would
be enhanced if it were to operate under the umbrella of a collective bargaining agreement between the faculty and the university.
As things stood, however, the frustrations of chapter members
were apparent in a statement that read:

It has become increasingly apparent that the Faculty Senate, as an advisory body, is not fully effective in securing implementation of its policies. Members of the Senate are increasingly recognizing this fact. The
Board of Trustees has dismissed Faculty Senate resolutions and Faculty
Senate representatives. It has been 2½ years since the Senate requested
the Board to endorse the 1966 AAUP *Statement on Government of Colleges
and Universities*. The Board has yet to reply to the Senate's request.[14]

The AAUP chapter also made it clear that it regarded the recent departure of Chancellor Oswald Tippo as a thinly veiled forced exit. Tippo had been a holdover from the years preceding Robert Wood's presidency, and he was often at odds with the new president.[15] According to the AAUP's line of thinking, the change in the chancellor's office was clear evidence of "bureaucratic centralized control and direction from the Boston office."[16] Related to this, one decision from Boston that particularly troubled faculty members concerned a proposed new tenure policy. Some faculty believed the change would pose a threat to non-tenured faculty members, which, at the time, constituted more than half the faculty.[17]

President Wood was the featured speaker at an AAUP chapter meeting in May 1972. In his remarks he addressed some of the governance issues that had been the source of difficulty during his tenure but, in general, he was optimistic about the future of the university. It was his view that many of these problems had been resolved. AAUP chapter members in attendance interpreted some of his remarks as indicating a somewhat favorable opinion on the issue of faculty collective bargaining.[18] Although some months later it would become evident that this assessment of Wood's thinking on this issue was probably mistaken, in the spring of 1972 AAUP chapter members saw little reason not to push forward with unionization plans. A similar assessment of the situation was made by the campus chapter of the Massachusetts Society of Professors.

An event in the fall of 1972 raised new concerns. Governor Sargent convened a joint meeting of all trustees of the state's institutions of higher education. The main purpose of this unusual meeting was to propose a comprehensive reorganization of public higher education in the state. Although some of those in the various public colleges and universities saw it differently, it appears that the impetus for the plan was motivated at least as much by economics as by politics. In fact, the plan to reorganize higher education was only a small part of a grander plan to reorganize the whole of state government. Sargent had taken the position that a comprehensive reorganization of state government would help to ease the state's serious fiscal situation and would, overall, streamline the somewhat-Byzantine arrangements that had

evolved over the years. When he met with the assembled trustees of the state institutions of higher learning, then, he intended
to begin the process of building support for a wholesale reorganization of public higher education.[19]
    The proposal was floated by Sargent and state Secretary of
Education Joseph Cronin. As one observer described it, the plan
called for:

> the University [of Massachusetts], the State Colleges, and the Commu-
> nity Colleges . . . [to be] placed under the direct administrative line au-
> thority of the Governor and his [sic] Secretary of Education, a political
> appointee.[20]

(A popular idea at the time nationally, the new entities were sometimes called "superboards.") This restructuring, Sargent claimed,
would "reconcile higher education with the cabinet form of government that now oversees every aspect of state administration."[21]
    One person in attendance at Sargent's meeting was Larry Ladd,
the president of the Student Government Association. His description of Sargent's proposal was widely circulated among the faculty in a newsletter from the Massachusetts Society of Professors.
The account raised several important issues in the minds of concerned professors. First, it seemed clear that this was not idle
speculation on the part of the governor, but rather an idea to
which he was firmly committed. In the course of his remarks to
the assembled trustees, however, other matters became apparent.
Of greatest concern was the issue of funding. Although it appeared that Sargent did not plan to propose outright cuts in higher
education spending, he did plan to seek level funding for higher
education in the coming budget. In a period of significant inflationary pressures, of course, it was apparent that this would
amount to a *de facto* decrease.[22]
    By this time, the Sargent administration had already been work-
ing on governmental restructuring in other areas of state operations. Based on this prior experience, the governor realized that
how he framed the higher education reorganization issue for public consumption would be important in achieving his goal. He also
knew that his proposal would meet with opposition. In seeking
comprehensive reform in the governance structure of public

higher education in the state, then, Sargent was eager to present his proposal in a way that would activate public support.

As a Republican governor in an overwhelmingly Democratic state, Sargent was accustomed to walking a fine line that sometimes brought fire from both parties. He harbored moderate views on many topics and usually adopted a pragmatist's approach to governmental problems. As a result, he was often at odds with Republican Party regulars, in addition to the more predictable difficulties he faced with the largely Democratic legislature. Outside government, one group with which he had a particularly troubled relationship was organized labor. Labor leaders and the governor were engaged in conflict almost from the first moment that Sargent entered the governor's office. He was surely aware that a proposal to reorganize the vast system of public higher education would likely prompt a reaction, and he needed to find a way to present his reorganization case in a way that would mute opposition.

In previous years, the national climate of student activism had shown political leaders that students could be a powerful source of political will in college and university life. In a public institution, the parents of students also represented a potential audience for higher education policy makers. Although ideology and protest against the Vietnam War motivated much student activism, there was another thematic strand running through rising student involvement on campus. This could be found in student demands for more relevance in courses and curricula—in other words, for a more student-centered focus to campus life. Sargent rhetorically connected his plan for reorganization to that impulse for a more powerful student focus in higher education, though his motivations were surely different from those of the student movement.

Sargent's description of the reorganization was couched in terms that linked his proposal restructing plan with broader reforms in educational practice. So, along with the implied efficiencies that a combined governing board allegedly would achieve, Sargent asserted that other outcomes—outcomes directly benefiting students—would be forthcoming as well. Prominent among these was to be a greater emphasis on teaching and, therefore, a relegation of faculty research to a secondary role. Indeed, Sargent seemed to have little use for a research-oriented professoriate and clearly favored a faculty geared almost exclusively toward teaching. (For good measure, it was suggested that the reorganization also would bring about a reduction in inflexible course requirements and the possibility of receiving credit for learning beyond the classroom.) It seemed, then, that Sargent's framing of the proposed reorganization was designed, in part, to arouse a sympathetic response from students, who were supposed to be its beneficiaries.[23]

A more skeptical assessment of the reorganization plan was possible, of course, and many in the UMass faculty took that less favorable view. From one faculty perspective, it seemed that the professors at UMass faced the possibility of more dramatic changes to their working lives than did faculties at the state colleges and community colleges. The research mission of a university was particularly at odds with the missions of other types of institutions. What the superboard approach seemed to promise was a conflation of the discrete assumptions and understandings about the various categories of institutions. The UMass faculty feared that the differing roles and missions of the state community colleges, four-year colleges, and universities would become homogenized and lost in Massachusetts.

Consider the different expectations about faculty work. Whereas a strong faculty time commitment to teaching could be seen as the norm at the community college level, a similar emphasis at the university level could only be achieved at the expense of research at the university. The question was not, as it was sometimes stated, whether teaching should constitute an important part of university life (since few would argue that teaching is not important), but rather what amount of teaching should be expected from a faculty whose members were engaged in research at the same time.

Sargent's comments seemed to suggest that recognition of the role of research in university life would be in jeopardy. In another sense, Sargent's proposition that teaching should be emphasized over research only repackaged the generally negative attitudes toward the research culture of university life that had been a commonplace feature of political rhetoric about education. By framing his reorganization proposal in this way and by linking it to popular student issues, Sargent was able to advance his proposal—and to cast criticism of it in a negative light—in one fell swoop. To argue against the reorganization would make the professors appear to be purveyors of self-interest and special privilege, not professionals who cared about student learning. At the outset, then, Sargent made a strong bid to control how debate about his proposal would be framed, making it an uphill battle for the professors to air objections that they may have had to the idea.

Given that the reorganization issue was raised in this way, it was not surprising that some members of the faculty saw a less-than-forthright motive behind Sargent's proposals. The official organ of the Massachusetts Society of Professors wrote:

> The Governor's concept of a university . . . is conditioned by politics, and above all he wishes to cut costs. The University, and public higher education in general, though comprising only about eight per cent of the state budget, has been chosen as a defenseless target. Only a united and politically effective stand by all elements of the community of higher education in the Commonwealth will suffice to withstand the great political pressures of the coming years.[24]

In this milieu, the issue of tenure also arose as a key concern of the faculty, especially when it came to be believed that the number of tenured faculty members would be capped by the administration. The substantive basis for such fear could be found in statements from administrative officials. For example, Robert L. Gluckstein, vice chancellor of academic affairs, wrote that ". . . it is likely that our institutional vigor cannot be maintained if we allow the present percentage (47%) [of tenured faculty] to grow much larger."[25] Although it is unclear if the administration was prepared to push this issue, the fact that it had any public airing at this time was sufficient to raise concerns in the faculty.

These apprehensions were exacerbated by a then–recent Supreme Court decision, *Regents v. Roth*. That decision seemed to limit a tenured faculty member's right to pursue court redress of non-appointment decisions under the Fourteenth Amendment. The Massachusetts Society of Professors stated:

> . . . the implications of *Roth* in conjunction with Governor Sargent's proposals are even more frightening. . . . Recent experience in the Common-

wealth, especially concerning the State College Governing Board, has shown that our present system is open to political interference. As an example, the Board of our University . . . has shown that it was prepared to ignore due process where expedient, resulting in long and bitter litigation for one of our colleagues."[26]

Such circumstances, sometimes seeming disparate, were coalescing to create an environment in which the idea of a faculty union looked increasingly attractive to many UMass faculty members. Many felt that they were bystanders in important university decisions. Salaries were leveling off even as inflation took hold. The state's financial situation was bleak, with dim prospects for a recovery anytime soon. The proposed reorganization presented the possibility that working arrangements could be altered. The tenure system seemed to be in a more precarious situation than had been the case in recent memory. Taken together, these circumstances caused many faculty members to conclude that their situation within the university was becoming tenuous.

Although pro-union sentiment was growing, there remained much uncertainty about whether this could be translated into the actual establishment of a formal union with collective bargaining rights. The idea of a labor union for the faculty was still a controversial idea, and many members of the faculty were skeptical that unionization would be a wise or appropriate response to recent developments.

In the pro-union camp, it also was becoming apparent that the presence of competing organizations could lead to disappointing results. The MSP and the AAUP chapter were actively promoting the faculty union solution, and the local AFT, though having less support, was also involved. Still, as unionization came to be discussed openly, the competition among the three groups was obvious and was noted in the news media, such as the *Boston Globe*.[27] The infighting among the groups, however, seemed to play into the hands of those who opposed unionization.

Already it seemed clear that the newly formed Massachusetts Society of Professors would play an important role in unfolding events. The local MSP was a newcomer at the university, but its parent organization, the Massachusetts Teachers Association, had provided resources for a full-time representative on the

UMass-Amherst campus.[28] Though its membership roster was initially smaller than that of the local AAUP chapter, it was growing, not only in numerical terms but also in influence. Some confrontation between the two groups seemed inevitable.

Seeking to navigate around the dangers posed by the sometimes- acrimonious competition between their two organizations and the possible damage that could result in the election, the local AAUP chapter and the MSP devised a "professional unity agreement" in early 1973.[29] Under the agreement, the two organizations would pool their efforts, thereby strengthening the chances that collective bargaining would be approved in the election. But this result would be achieved in such a way that each of the faculty organizations would remain more or less intact. The agreement called for the Massachusetts Teachers Association to fill the role of the bargaining agent if collective bargaining were adopted. This resolution to the competition between the two groups was highly unusual. The fact that it was proposed at all, however, indicated that the groups were well aware that excessive zeal in their rivalry could be damaging to their cause and might result in outright failure at the ballot box.

In announcing this new strategy, a joint MSP-AAUP memorandum urged faculty members to join one of the two groups if they had not already done so. They reached broadly in soliciting new members. They appealed to professors at all ranks, as would be expected, but also to instructors, librarians (holding ranks I through V), department chairpersons, and various program directors. There was no certainty at the time that all these groups would be recognized as legitimate members in an as-yet-undetermined bargaining-unit. For the time being, however, the two groups decided to cast the net as widely as seemed feasible, leaving final adjudication about bargaining unit eligibility to future determination by the Massachusetts Labor Relations Commission, the governing authority for the public-sector labor relations in the state.

The mechanics of the proposed MSP-AAUP combination showed efforts to strike a balance power acceptable to each of the rival groups. When the combination group was first announced, final details had yet to be worked out. However, the groups had given thought to how the efforts of the groups could be combined without dismantling either one. At the general membership level AAUP and MSP cardholders would be considered members of a proposed General Assembly. It would be this new body that would hold the power to ratify any collective bargaining agreement. At the leadership level, however, power would be concentrated in the MSP. In a proposed ten-member executive council, seven of the members were to come from the MSP and the remaining three from the AAUP. It was agreed that in future years that proportion would be readjusted to reflect changes in membership levels in the two groups.[30]

Though the two groups were still negotiating the details of their association, activities directed at their common goal of organizing the faculty accelerated. The MSP formally made its intention to begin a union drive known in mid-February of 1973. As reported in a bylined article in the *Boston Globe*, the MSP effort was largely coordinated with help from MSP's parent organization, the MTA.[31] The state office provided organizers and funding for the effort. Though MTA officials disputed the figure, it was reported that as much as $100,000 would be forthcoming from the state office for the efforts at Amherst.[32]

Word of the group's intentions spread. The *Boston Globe*, for example, continued to follow the developments. In the following month, a headline characterized the MSP efforts as the "Labor movement comes to UMass."[33] (The account again repeated the alleged budget of $100,000 from the MTA that had been reported earlier.) By this time, various constituencies were responding to the unionization bid, and these were recounted in the press, drawing the lines of confrontation that would characterize the entire campaign. A leader of the student senate was quoted as stating that a faculty union would "hurt students."[34] It was reported that Robert Gluckstein, the vice chancellor for academic affairs, stated that he was "not attracted to the notion that faculty concerns can be better served by unionization."[35]

Work on the organizing effort moved along quickly. By early March, the MSP petitioned the Massachusetts Labor Relations Commission to set a date for an election. Though some technical problems in the manner in which the materials were submitted caused some delay,[36] a fall election looked likely.

At this point, the paperwork was filed by the MSP without inclusion of its "unity" partner, the local AAUP chapter, but the two organizations continued their joint efforts to build support for a union. Among the first joint MSP-AAUP activities was a plan to organize debates on the merits of collective bargaining. As part of these initiatives, MSP-AAUP leaders asked some department chairs to convene meetings in which the respective department members could discuss the collective bargaining issue. These requests elicited a quick response from Gluckstein.

In a letter sent to deans, department chairs, and directors, Gluckstein warned that granting the MSP-AAUP request could result in the university violating the Commonwealth's labor laws. Stating that the university's counsel had so advised, Gluckstein told the chairs to deny all such requests from MSP-AAUP.[37] (Driving home this point, the next day another memorandum was issued in which it was firmly stated that scheduled classes or related academic activities were not to be cancelled for the purposes of providing opportunities for faculty to debate the collective bargaining issue.[38]) These administrative responses were grounded in the complexities of labor law, stipulating which activities could or could not be legally undertaken. The tone of these communications, however, exacerbated the contentious feelings that had already surfaced in some quarters of the faculty.

In future weeks, the disagreements between union supporters and the administration were further heightened. One troublesome topic was the continuing dispute about whether or not department chairpersons would be included as part of the proposed bargaining unit.

During this same period, in the spring of 1973, a new governance proposal for the university emerged.[39] Devised by a group of professors and administrators, it sought to placate the concerns of both faculty and students. Robert Wellman, a well-respected professor in the School of Education, headed the group. The plan, which was approved by the board of trustees in April, emphasized that faculty and student views would be included in university decision making. Wellman and the other architects of the plan saw it providing a mechanism that would bring together the voices of the various constituencies within the university. There were already very mixed feelings among the faculty regarding the desirability of collective bargaining, and the Wellman plan seems to have further been cause for many faculty members to step back from the idea of unionization. It seemed to provide a way to resolve some of the current tensions without taking the momentous step of adopting collective bargaining.

Still, salary issues remained an important concern for pro-union faculty members in Amherst. Public sympathy for their situation was surely undercut, however, by the May publication of a newspaper report on that issue. The study reported that, in a ten-year period, the average salary of a UMass faculty member had doubled and that, on average, faculty pay was well above the national median.[40] The report was originally part of series appearing in the mid-state *Daily Hampshire Gazette*. However, it was subsequently distributed by the Associated Press and was quoted in both the *Boston Globe* and the *Boston Herald*, thereby giving the information much wider exposure than might otherwise have been the case.

On campus, the supporters of a faculty union continued to encounter opposition from student leaders. Students feared that in a collective bargaining relationship between the faculty and the administration, they would be the losers. Wary of being shut out of important campus decisions, they editorialized against a faculty union.

When the faculty returned to campus in the fall of 1973, it was by no means clear that a vote on collective bargaining would be won by the pro-union camp. This was not always apparent in the public statements of faculty and administrative leaders. The tone of their rhetoric took on an increasingly dramatic air. Officially, and in line with state law on the matter, the administration took a neutral position. The chancellor at Amherst was quoted as stating:

Our position has been that the faculty should make its decision on this vital question based on fact and reason, rather than emotion, realizing that it may be the single most important decision that the faculty has been required to make. . . . While we believe that collective bargaining is a backward move for faculty participation in campus governance and is contrary to the best interest of the faculty and the whole University, this is an issue that the faculty itself must resolve on the basis of the best information available and sensitive consideration to the profound long-term implications.[41]

Still, by the fall there had been sufficient progress on the contested aspects of the collective bargaining election to enable the Massachusetts Labor Relations Commission to set a date for a vote on the matter in early November. On October 25, 1973, the Labor Relations Commission of the Commonwealth of Massachusetts announced that parties had agreed to an election concerning representation.[42] Though the inclusion of some groups (such as chairpersons) in the proposed bargaining unit was still unresolved, it was agreed that the election could go forward and that a determination on contested ballots could be resolved at a later date.

The acrimony between the MSP-AAUP coalition and the administration reached its apex in the days before the scheduled election. When it was reported that an unidentified group had engaged the services of a polling firm to gauge the support for unionization within the faculty, the administration cried foul. Administration officials asserted that if it were shown that either the MSP or the AAUP had been responsible for this action, it would have constituted an unlawful interference in the campaign process. Despite some acrimonious rhetoric, the process did not stop, however, and the election went forward.

The faculty voted on November 15 and 16, 1973. It had been a long campaign, and Eduard Robreno, the lead organizer assigned by the Massachusetts Teachers Association to the case, predicted a favorable vote on unionization.[43] But the campaign had been bitter, and many members of the faculty remained unsure about the idea of unionization. Moreover, the Wellman proposal had resulted in a newly negotiated understanding with the Board of Trustees, which seemed to offer solutions to faculty issues without requiring the bigger step of collective bargaining. Though there was considerable support for unionization, the campus faculty was still very much divided on the issue.

When the votes from the election were tallied, then, 1,404 votes were cast (about two-thirds of those eligible), with 718 against collective bargaining and 510 in favor. Another 174 votes, which were contested by the university, were not included in the tally, but this was a moot point since the contested votes could not have altered the outcome.[44]

Later, the local AAUP chapter presented the following analysis of what had transpired:

The reasons [for the 1973 vote of "no agent"] were many. A new governance procedure had just been negotiated with the Board of Trustees and many felt it deserved a full and fair trial. Many faculty members had reservations about the MSP/MTA-AAUP coalition as their agent. For a number of faculty, a union was incompatible with academe."[45]

Frustrated by this failure, the differences between the MSP and AAUP resurfaced, and their alliance largely fell apart. For the moment, it seemed that the Wellman proposal and other recent developments had the potential to soothe faculty concerns. The unionization effort had revealed deep cleavages within the faculty, and the future prospects for building majority support for a faculty union anytime soon looked remote.

THE SECOND CAMPAIGN

Although it appeared that the idea of establishing a faculty union at UMass had been put to rest, the issue resurfaced less than two years later. In many ways, this second unionization bid was a more complex affair than the first effort, and the influence of external politics was more pronounced. Simultaneous streams of events that came together rekindled unionism among the UMass faculty. The most significant of these were the deepening state fiscal crisis and political ramifications from it, the arrival of a new governor who would publicly clash with the UMass president, and a continuing deterioration of relations between the university administration and the faculty. An examination of these overlapping stories contributes to an understanding of how the faculty came to reverse course.

Within two years many circumstances would change. One important shift that had occurred was related to the state labor law covering public employees. Under new provisions in Massachusetts General Laws, Chapter 150E, state employees were given expanded rights in collective bargaining. Most important, the law granted the right to bargain over wages, a key aspect of the law— and an important potential selling point for pro-unionists—that was previously absent.[46]

State politics exerted a profound influence over the circumstances that led to a second faculty unionization attempt at

UMass. In the state political arena, Michael S. Dukakis was sworn into office in January of 1975, returning control of the governor's office to the Democrats. The fact that one party now controlled state government did not result, however, in a lack of conflict in state policy making. The legislative leadership showed little interest in relinquishing power and deferring to the new governor. The magnitude of the fiscal situation soon weighed heavily on the new governor. In March, Dukakis noted that Massachusetts was in the "worst economic recession" since before the Second World War. With a deficit on one hand and a constitutional obligation to balance the state budget on the other, Dukakis was looking for options.[47]

In May of 1975, Governor Dukakis and his secretary of education, Paul Parks, journeyed to Amherst to make their case for a 10 percent cut in public higher education in the next budget. According to one press estimate, about 2,500 students and onlookers turned out to hear what Dukakis and Parks had to say, though it was clear that many did not expect to hear news that would please them.[48] As Dukakis attempted to outline his analysis of the state's budget problems and his proposals to alleviate them, he was confronted with audience chants of "no more budget cuts" and a series of questions from the audience that a reporter characterized as "increasingly hostile."[49]

On the UMass campus, a new policy that was announced in the 1974–75 academic year had already heightened uneasiness about the future relationship between the faculty and the administration. The MSP reported with concern that "the traditional role of Department Head/Chairman as an advocate for the faculty will be eliminated"; these positions were to be redesignated "departmental administrative officers," which "by implication . . . [would] make them] agents of the administration."[50]

More significantly, little progress had been made on faculty salary issues. With public higher education under continued budgetary pressure, there was increasing frustration within the faculty. Soon, support for the idea of organizing a new bid for collective bargaining began to grow. The MSP began to work toward this end in the spring of 1975.[51] Though there seemed to be sufficient support to at least petition the state for a second election, there would be a considerable delay before that was to occur. Over the coming months, there would be battles with the administration over who would be included in a unit—again hinging largely on the status of department chairpersons—and on the matter of forming a combined bargaining unit with the newer Boston campus of the university. As the process stretched out, the opportunities for acrimony came more frequently.

To make matters worse, because of ongoing state fiscal problems, it was reported that the powerful president of the Massachusetts Senate, Kevin B. Harrington, had suggested that there was a possibility that UMass might be closed for the spring semester.[52] Though Harrington may have been misinterpreted, members of the faculty increasingly were concerned about matters in their day-to-day life on campus. The prospect of cuts in a wide range of services affecting faculty was viewed with some alarm. Such concerns, combined with the ongoing salary issue, created a troubled environment that was apparent to all. Reporting some months later, the chancellor of the Amherst campus candidly wrote :

We accepted the challenge to accommodate the campus to the reductions caused by adverse economic conditions in the Commonwealth. The cost was high, though; average class size and faculty workloads increased significantly at a time when, because of legislation passed in the General Court, we were unable to grant our faculty and professional staff either cost-of-living or merit increases. As a consequence, campus morale was low.[53]

TENSIONS BETWEEN THE GOVERNOR AND THE UNIVERSITY

Some members of the faculty were critical of the central administration, and more of them began to reconsider unionization. Meanwhile, a negative view of the university administration had been developing in the state executive branch. Spending at the university was an ongoing source of aggravation in the Dukakis administration. In the summer of 1975, for example, it had become known that the chancellor at Amherst, Randolph W. Bromery, had billed the state for a number of flights between Amherst and Boston. Ostensibly, these flights enabled Bromery to make more efficient use of his time on those occasions when he traveled to the state capital to conduct university business. It made a poor impression in the press, however. Attempting to explain the situation, Bromery reported that "I know that some taxpayers will be bothered by the appearance of the flights. If I thought that the impact were unfavorable to the university, I wouldn't do it."[54] Dukakis apparently found little comfort in this explanation. The governor's press secretary characterized the flights as "outrageous at best," further stating that "I find it difficult to believe that there were 21 occasions of such dire emergency that he would have to fly to Boston."[55]

The governor's displeasure with the university did not end there, however. Just as the university had resisted requests for budget cuts from Dukakis's predecessor, university officials held their ground with the new administration. Dukakis had asked the university to work up a budget in the range of $91 million. UMass President Wood paid little attention to that request. He stated that the university would decline "to participate in an artificial budget exercise."[56] Emphasizing his position, he added, "I did not agree to engage in institutional hara-kiri."[57] Instead, when he appeared before the House Ways and Means Committee, Wood said he "could live with" a budget of about $103 million.[58]

The budgetary dispute exacerbated already apparent strains in the relationship between the university president and the governor. A frustrated Dukakis stated, "I don't think the university understands the enormity of the problem. The president of the university has not chosen to sit down with the secretary of educational affairs to discuss this matter openly and fully, despite repeated requests to do so."[59] Although Dukakis publicly stated that he "liked" Wood and was "not interested in pitched battles," the friction between the two men was obvious. The Boston press commented on it and speculated that as soon as Dukakis appointees were sufficiently numerous to constitute a majority on the university's board of trustees, the administration would apply pressure to have Wood removed from his post. Overseeing a state with many fiscal problems and facing battles on many fronts, however, Dukakis surely realized that Wood's political savvy and strong links to the legislature would make him a formidable opponent in any public row. The governor proceeded cautiously in the following months.

By the fall of 1975 and in office less than a year, the Democratic governor found himself in a very public dispute with Kevin B. Harrington, the Democratic president of the Massachusetts Senate. Harrington had proposed to reorganize the state's higher education system along the lines of a "superboard," a plan that was quite similar to the failed plan that had been advanced by Francis Sargent a few years earlier. Governor Dukakis did not favor this approach. He instead preferred the compromise of a "coordinating board" and had submitted that alternative to the legislature.[60]

The conflict later became complicated and more overtly political. Matters undoubtedly were exacerbated by the fact that, in exploring the possibility of reorganization, Harrington appeared to be working closely with the UMass president. Opposition to the superboard plan grew, with opponents—among them, the governor, the MSP, the MTA, and the AAUP—fighting it vigorously in the legislature. By June of 1976, the *Boston Globe* would report:

[Harrington's] grand design to reorganize public higher education—and in the process upstage Gov. Michael S. Dukakis—is slowly coming apart. . . . Dukakis and his ad hoc legislative allies are concerned that the strong governing board envisioned by Harrington and Wood would take away from the legislature's own budget authority. . . . State House skeptics . . . cannot shake the feeling that Harrington and Wood have a personal stake in the passage of the reorganization plan.[61]

Indeed, the many protests elicited by the proposal, combined with the opposition of the governor, led Harrington to drop the plan altogether.

STATE-EMPLOYEE LABOR CRISIS

Considered independently, the controversy about governance in higher education may seem to be an unremarkable political battle, not unlike routine business in state politics. For the Dukakis administration, however, the episode had connections to a larger problem. Complicating matters for the governor's administration was the fact that the reorganization proposal, which had been vigorously opposed by the major teacher and faculty organizations, occurred in the context of already contentious relations with many other segments of the state's public work force. Indeed, the administration was already expending significant energy in trying to keep state relations with its vocal and unhappy employees from over-boiling. Since the start of his term, the fragile relationship between Dukakis and labor leaders in the state had deteriorated. During his first weeks in office in 1975, the governor met with state-employee leaders, and he had attempted to form at least a modest alliance with them as he looked for ways out of the budget crisis.[62] State payrolls were a large part of the budget, and he wanted to avoid layoffs. Only a year later, however, as the fight over reorganizing higher education continued, the Boston news media reported that organized labor was "alienated" from the governor. One union official stated that "We're disgusted with the performance of the administration."[63] Stagnant salaries were a major concern of nearly all state workers, and relations between a coalition of state-employee unions and the Dukakis administration soured.

By June of 1976, the level of frustration among state workers had reached the boiling point, and the union coalition called for a strike, a move that would violate state law. The level of unhappiness about salary proposals was high, however, and the strike went forward, affecting such operations as prisons, mental hospitals, bridges, and water-treatment plants. The three-day strike, which ended only minutes before a fine of $200,000 per day was to be instituted, was unsettling for the administration. Subsequently, a mediator raised the salary figures slightly from the state's proposal, and the governor issued an amnesty for those who had participated in the strike.[64] The strike by thousands of public employees posed a serious challenge to the Dukakis administration, however, and one that showed the potential for political fallout in the months to come.

The relationship between labor—especially state-employee labor groups—and the administration remained tenuous. It also remained a hot topic in the Boston news media. By the fall, Wilfrid C. Rodgers, who covered labor issues for the Boston Globe, wrote that Dukakis "finds himself deeper in labor's doghouse than any Bay State governor since . . . 1947. . . . To understand why, one must look at the rise of the fastest growing part of the labor movement—public workers."[65] By this time, UMass professors had increasingly turned to unionism, and there can have been little enthusiasm within the governor's office for a confrontation with yet another group of state employees.

Meanwhile, strains between Dukakis and Wood resurfaced. In addition to allying himself with the senate president and against Dukakis in the reorganization scheme, UMass President Robert Wood had successfully persuaded the legislature to restore budget cuts that the Dukakis administration had submitted. The *Boston Globe* reported that Wood had used the services of three lobbyists at the State House to achieve this outcome. This was clearly a source of annoyance for Dukakis. His general frustration with UMass could be detected in published comments:

I'm obviously not happy with what I've seen there partly because I've seen the development of what I think is an extremely expensive and not terribly effective central office.

I don't think it's a very happy system. You could sense that from the statement the other day of the faculty on the whole superboard concept. It was not very subtle in terms of what it was talking about, whom it was directed at.[66]

The icy relationship between the governor and the university president prevailed for some months.[67]

RENEWED SUPPORT FOR UNIONIZATION ON CAMPUS

During the months that these events were unfolding in the state capital, work toward a second collective bargaining election had been making substantial progress in Amherst. A year earlier, in 1975, leaders of the MSP and local AAUP chapter had become increasingly optimistic about a second union bid. From their perspective, the reasons to pursue the unionization option had grown stronger.

In this campaign, however, they sought the right to represent the faculty independently, leading to an ongoing competition. For example, in late 1975 rumors had circulated about the viability of the AAUP chapter as a collective bargaining agent. In response, a notice was issued stating that "AAUP is neither broke or without legal counsel. National AAUP has made a substantial direct grant of money to the Chapter to assist our collective bargaining effort." To bolster its case, it fired off a salvo against the MSP and its parent organization, the state NEA affiliate, asserting that "It goes without saying that our lawyer is totally involved in higher education and not diverted with the problems of grades K-12 in the public schools!"[68] Though both groups favored a union, neither was keen to see the other as the bargaining agent.

One issue that had gained increased attention was the question of whether the Amherst and Boston campuses should be treated separately or as a combined bargaining unit. Though there was support among the faculty for establishing separate bargaining units, MSP and AAUP leaders recognized that the university leadership was apt to view the situation otherwise. In May 1975, the Massachusetts Labor Relations Commission had ruled that the state's community colleges were to be treated as one bargaining unit, rather than as separate entities. With that precedent, MSP and AAUP leaders believed that a fight for separate Amherst and Boston units would result in a protracted legal battle. To expedite the bid for unionization, MSP and AAUP leaders agreed that they would not contest the matter.[69]

A year later, in the spring of 1976, the budget crisis at UMass-Amherst remained a source of unrest within the faculty. Some believed that administrative decisions had made matters worse. One school of thought traced part of the problem to the purported diversion of funds from core university services to the central office in Boston.[70] Meanwhile, it seemed that the faculty would be asked to make a choice between giving up telephones or secretarial assistance.[71]

The AAUP chapter pushed the salary issue throughout this time. Its September newsletter asserted that faculty salaries at the university had continued to decline when measured against national rankings. The upshot of this, it was claimed, would be that UMass would face increasing difficulties in recruiting and retaining top faculty members.[72]

In October of 1976, the Massachusetts Labor Relations Commission finally ordered a new election to determine whether collective bargaining would be instituted at the university. The commission had ruled that department heads, chairpersons, and librarians would be included in the election and would be entitled to representation, a decision that the AAUP chapter characterized as "a clear defeat for the administration's lawyers."[73]

CAMPAIGN RHETORIC

The rhetoric surrounding the campaign centered on familiar themes. "To our dismay," the local AAUP wrote, "we find the central administration unwilling to support the shared responsibility and collegial atmosphere we sought via the established and familiar framework."[74] Writing for the MSP, another faculty member had already outlined the arguments in favor of a union. First, it was again asserted that the faculty had little influence on campus and that the administration did not pay much attention to it. The suggestion was that because, under law, it had no requirement to consider the faculty's sentiment on various matters, the administration did not do so. To the MSP, it seemed that the administration was not willing to engage in a constructive dialogue with the faculty. Therefore, unionization and collective bargaining were seen as developments that would compel administrative leaders to pay greater attention to the faculty. In addition to providing ostensible benefits to the faculty, the MSP argument favoring unionization also suggested that these changes would enhance the workings of the administration, though precisely how was not specified.[75]

As the campaign became more heated, opinions about the unionization question were forthcoming from an increasing number of sources, both within the faculty and from the administration. Arguing that a union would prove to be detrimental, some opponents adopted a tack that stressed the potential tensions between individual interests and group interests that are inherent in collective action. For example, the provost contended that "salary equalization proposals"—examples of which had recently been proposed at Florida State University—"constituted a system of *salary redistribution*, [emphasis in original] a form of 'income transfer among members of the faculty. With this system, there must be losers.'"[76]

Another complaint about the prospect of unionization held that a unionized faculty would result in a loss of both the collegiality and the sense of community in the university that was said to have existed. Typically, it was claimed by union opponents (including administrators and anti-union faculty) that the tensions between management and workers found in the unionized industrial sector would be transferred to the university. The faculty was also cautioned that unionization would not lead to the results that they sought.

These were among the warnings contained in a memorandum sent by the academic deans to the faculty in November of 1976. In the month before the scheduled election, they voiced reservations about the possibility of faculty unionization.[77] The deans suggested that a union would threaten the caliber of education at the university by prompting many of the strongest faculty members to leave the university. The deans asserted that UMass had only lately come to be regarded as a school of quality, and that this was precisely because it had been successful in attracting top-flight faculty members and had instituted meritocratic procedures in recruiting and promoting faculty. A union would hamper the university's ability to make such individual judgments, and an aura of mediocrity would set in.[78]

In addition, the deans made the argument that a union might irreparably harm the collegial environment that it thought existed on campus. They apparently envisioned an antagonistic management-labor relationship, especially if department chairs were members of the bargaining unit. In addition to that unhappy state of affairs, they thought that the legitimate authority of individual schools and committees would be seriously threatened.[79]

At the same time, UMass President Robert Wood warned faculty that unionization was unlikely to result in more funding for the university, stating that "certainly, no such result has occurred within the Commonwealth," a reference to already unionized campuses elsewhere in the state higher education system. He added that any ideas that faculty had about a union dealing with the administration over general governance and policy issues were, in his view, mistaken. Wood stated:

It is our opinion . . . that the University is not obligated to deal with the union with respect to any questions of faculty governance, or faculty participation and voice in University affairs outside the ambit of the mandatory subjects [e.g., wages, hours, standards of productivity and performance].[80]

The same line comes through in documents produced by other administrative officials. The provost, for example, issued a statement to the faculty in which it was stated that "the adversarial nature of collective bargaining will require that officials assume a more traditional management posture in dealing with faculty (labor)" [parentheses in original].[81]

Many of the arguments against a union emphasized the qualitative difference that a unionized environment would bring. The assumption was that this difference would be negative. The presumption seemed to be that a sense of collegiality and community were the norm on campus. After all, one presumably would not lament the loss of something that did not exist. The substantive basis for this belief may have been lost in the rhetoric, however. In fact, many members of the faculty did not share these assumptions.

If administrative leaders believed that a sense of collegiality was so widely shared among the faculty that linking a union to its loss could successfully persuade the faculty to abandon unionization, they would soon find out that this was not the case. The counterclaim had been made that an adversarial relationship between the faculty and administration would not newly emerge from the adoption of unionization because a negative relationship already existed. This, it was asserted, had been the case since the departure of Oswald Tippo from the chancellor's office several years earlier.[82] The central administration in Boston was "insensitive" to faculty concerns and more interested in itself, the argument went. The administration in Amherst was said to be weak and had done little to better the faculty's situation, particularly in obtaining cost-of-living increases.[83]

Of course, though unionism had grown in strength, many members of the faculty still did not agree with the idea of collective bargaining. A group of about twenty-five faculty members, calling themselves the Committee for Informed Faculty, came together and made the case against unionization. Commenting to a reporter from the campus newspaper, the group's leader, a professor of Spanish, stated that the group was "trying to prevent the union movement if possible. We feel people are not really seeing the facts because they are being fed propaganda by the two groups vying to represent faculty in collective bargaining."[84] One of the group's basic arguments was that unions were incompatible with academe. It was suggested that a union would lead to "mediocrity."[85] A flyer distributed by the group declared, "A university, not a factory!"[86]

At the last minute, a proposal from Wood to raise the salaries of nonprofessional workers at the university created yet another controversy. The Massachusetts Teachers Association saw this development as an inappropriate intrusion into the imminent vote on faculty collective bargaining. The executive director of the MTA told the press, "President Wood is guilty of the crudest form of interference," [87] but the affair seems to have had little effect on the outcome of the election. It did, however, serve to further harden the attitudes between union organizers and the president's office.

ELECTION SUCCESS

In the end, the arguments against unionization did not dissuade a majority of the faculty of the combined campuses from favoring collective bargaining. Nonetheless, the election in December 1976 ended with no choice receiving more than 50 percent of the vote. The MSP–Faculty Staff Union received 810 votes, far more than any other option. However, the MSP-FSU vote resulted in a plurality only, since the AAUP had received 268 votes and 580 votes were cast against collective bargaining altogether.[88] (There were also 147 challenged ballots.) With no choice meeting the requirement of more than 50 percent, a runoff election was scheduled for February.

The runoff election two months later elicited less acrimony and controversy. With the options limited to the top two choices from the previous ballot, the results of the runoff were 865 in favor of choosing the MSP-FSU as the collective bargaining agent and 680 voting against collective bargaining. (The number of challenged votes was now reduced to 74, with an additional 2 ballots submitted blank.[89]) By this time, the campus was clearly weary from two protracted unionization campaigns. Still, the central administration seemed to only grudgingly accept the decision to adopt collective bargaining, and much of the bitterness produced by the campaign would be evident in both camps for some time to come.

NOTES

1. David Riesman and Christopher Jencks, "The Viability of the American College," in *The American College*, ed. Sanford Nevitt (New York: Wiley & Sons, 1962), 138.

2. See Harold Whiting Cary, *The University of Massachusetts: A History of One Hundred Years* (Amherst: University of Massachusetts, 1962), 173–74.

3. Ibid., 201–2.

4. Edgar Litt, *Political Cultures of Massachusetts* (Cambridge: MIT Press, 1965), 177–79.

5. Ibid., 179.

6. Ibid., 178.

7. Tom Juravich, William F. Hartford, and James R. Green, *Commonwealth of Toil: Chapters in the History of Massachusetts Workers and Their Unions.* (Amherst: University of Massachusetts Press, 1996), 140–41.

8. To complicate matters, Sargent was not originally elected to the governor's office, but rather was elected lieutenant governor. He was elevated to the higher office when Governor John Volpe accepted a cabinet position in the Nixon administration.

9. Quoted in James Worsham, "Carnegie hones ax, Sargent swings it," *Boston Sunday Globe*, 10 September, 1972.

10. See Richard M. Freeland, *Academia's Golden Age: Universities in Massachusetts, 1945–1970* (New York: Oxford University Press, 1992).

11. "Unionization concerns question of faculty role," *Daily Hampshire Gazette*, 19 April 1973.

12. *AAUP Newsletter, University of Massachusetts Chapter*, 2:1 (November 1971). (Located in the University Archives, W.E.B. Du Bois Library, University of Massachusetts at Amherst, hereafter referred to as UMA.)

13. *AAUP Newsletter, University of Massachusetts Chapter*, 2:2 (January, 1972), UMA.

14. Ibid.

15. See Freeland.

16. *AAUP Newsletter, University of Massachusetts Chapter*, 2:2 (January, 1972), UMA.

17. Ibid., 2.

18. UMass-AAUP, Minutes of meeting, 12 May 1972, UMA.

19. *MasSProf Newsletter* [*sic*], n.d. [1972b]), UMA.

20. Ibid.

21. *MaSProf Newsletter*, n.d. [1972]), UMA.

22. Massachusetts Society of Professors, Memorandum to faculty, n.d. [November 1972], UMA.

23. Ibid.

24. *MaSProf Newsletter*, n.d. [1972], UMA.

25. Robert L. Gluckstein, Memorandum, 15 November 1971, UMA.

26. *MaSProf Newsletter*, n.d. [1972], UMA.

27. "3 UMass faculty unions vie for bargaining power," *Boston Globe*, 6 October 1972.

28. Ibid.

29. Massachusetts Society of Professors and the American Association of University Professors, UMass-Amherst Chapter, Memorandum to the faculty, [undated, circa January 1973], UMA.

30. Ibid.

31. David Nyhan, "Union drive at UMass," *Boston Globe*, 14 February 1973.

32. Ibid.

33. William Densmore, "Labor movement comes to UMass," *Boston Sunday Globe*, 25 March 1973.

34. Ibid.

35. Ibid.

36. "UMass faculty unit seeks vote on bargaining," *Boston Globe*, 9 March 1973.

37. Robert L. Gluckstein, Memorandum to deans, directors, department heads and chairmen [*sic*], April 19, 1973, UMA.

38. Robert L. Gluckstein, Memorandum to deans, directors, department heads and chairmen [*sic*], April 20, 1973, UMA.

39. At this time there were three campuses of the university: the flagship Amherst campus, plus a campus in Boston and the medical campus in Worcester.

40. See "UMass faculty paid $4000 more than national median," *Boston Globe*, 16 May 1973, and "UMass Professor [*sic*] Salary Doubled Over 10 Years," *Boston Herald*, 16 May 1973.

41. Quoted in Richard Lemere, "UMass Faculty Eyes Union," *Herald Sunday Advertiser*, 16 September 1973.

42. Commonwealth of Massachusetts, Before the Labor Relations Commission, "Notice of Election," 25 October 1973, UMA.

43. See David Nyhan, "UMass faculty votes on union," *Boston Globe*, 16 November 1973.

44. Ibid.

45. AAUP-UMass Chapter, Memorandum, 1976, 15 November 1976.

46. See Juravich, Hartford, and Green, 142.

47. Rachelle Patterson, "Labor leaders stress need for jobs," *Boston Sunday Globe*, 23 March 1975.

48. George Briggs and Ed O'Connor, "Dukakis Gives Crash $$ [*sic*] Course at UMass," *Boston Herald*, 6 May 1975.

49. William Densmore, Jr., "Dukakis takes case to students," *Boston Globe*, 6 May 1975.

50. Massachusetts Society of Professors, Memorandum to faculty, 22 February 1975, UMA.

51. Massachusetts Society of Professors, Memorandum to the faculty, 5 May 1975, UMA.

52. AAUP-UMass Chapter, Executive Committee, Minutes, 7 November 1975, UMA.

53. Office of the Chancellor, University of Massachusetts, Amherst, Annual Report, 1976, UMA.

54. See "Dukakis hits Chancellor's Flights," *Boston Herald*, 9 August 1975.

55. Ibid.

56. See "Dukakis blames UMass president for differences in budget requests," *Boston Globe*, 9 August 1975.

57. Ibid.

58. Ibid.

59. Ibid.

60. AAUP-UMass Newsletter, 29 April 1976.

61. M. Kenney, "Harrington's plan falling apart," *Boston Globe*, 29 June 1976.

62. George B. Merry, "Dukakis to meet with state-union heads," *Christian Science Monitor*, 16 January 1975.

63. Richard Lamere, "Unions alienated by Dukakis," *Boston Herald*, 4 April 1976.

64. These events were covered in the *New York Times*, which published various accounts between June 21 and June 27, 1976.

65. Wilfrid C. Rodgers, "Dukakis in the doghouse," *Boston Globe*, 18 September 1976.

66. "Dukakis preparing to oust UMass president," *Boston Globe*, 22 July 1976.

67. Carol Surkin, "Dukakis-Wood rift seems to be healing," *Boston Globe*, 2 December 1976. By late 1976, however, it began to thaw. At that point, Dukakis's appointees had taken a dominant role on the university's board of trustees, but it seemed increasingly evident that Dukakis would not attempt to oust Wood from office. By December of 1976—just as the UMass faculty was preparing to vote on the question of collective bargaining—the two men appeared to have reached some level of understanding that could lead to a more peaceful coexistence.

68. AAUP, UMass Chapter, Notice circulated to faculty, 4 December 1975, UMA.

69. In the matter of establishing combined or separate bargaining units, it is interesting to note that the university administration did not pursue the matter of including all faculties of the university into one bargaining unit. While they pushed for a combination of Amherst and Boston, it appears that little serious thought was given to adding the medical school faculty of the Worcester campus to the combined group. Though the national phenomenon of faculty unionization in higher education was still relatively new, there was already sufficient evidence to suggest that the faculties of medical schools seemed less likely to embrace unionization. The ethos of collective bargaining had little in common with the values and self-perception of members of the medical profession at that time. It would seem, therefore, that the addition of a medical school faculty to the faculties of the two traditional campuses in Amherst and Boston likely would have had the effect of increasing the tally of negative votes in a combined-unit election concerning collective bargaining. For reasons that are not clear, however, the matter was not pursued, resulting in a proposed unit consisting only of the Amherst and Boston campuses.

70. See "Bargaining Activity," *Academe* 10:1 (1976): 9.

71. Ibid.

72. AAUP, UMass Chapter, Memorandum, 7 September 1976, UMA.

73. AAUP, UMass Chapter, Newsletter, 18 October 1976, UMA.

74. AAUP-UMass Chapter, Minutes, 15 November 1976, UMA.

75. See I. P. Rothberg, Memorandum (ca. 1976), UMA.

76. P. Puryear, Letter to faculty, 17 November 1976, UMA.

77. L.O. Wilkinson, J. Marcus, G. Craig, J. Hart, S. Shapiro, D. Bischoff, R. Whaley, E. Fellar, G. Odiorne, Memorandum to faculty, 18 November 1976, UMA.

78. Ibid.

79. Ibid.

80. Robert Wood, Letter to faculty, 22 November 1976, UMA.

81. Puryear, 17 November 1976, UMA.

82. Rothberg, ca. 1976, UMA.

83. Ibid.

84. See Lisa Mellili, "Group Against Bargaining," *The Collegian*, 19 November 1976, UMA.

85. Committee for Informed Faculty, Memorandum to the faculty, 24 November 1976, UMA.

86. Ibid.

87. Frank Thompson, "Wood hit as union meddler," *Boston Herald*, 1 December 1976.

88. "UMass union vote unclear; faculty agrees to runoff," *Boston Globe*, 4 December 1976.

89. "2 UMass staffs vote to unionize," *Boston Globe*, 12 February 1977.

CHAPTER 6

Faculty Unionization at the University of Connecticut

Like its neighbor to the north, Connecticut is home to many institutions of higher education, the most notable of which is ven-
erable Yale University in the southeastern city of New Haven.
Yale's longevity, international reputation, and location in a quad-
rant of the state that is only a short distance from New York City
have insured its prominence. In the opposite corner of the state,
amid rolling hills and farmlands, lies the state's flagship public
institution of higher learning, the University of Connecticut
(UConn). From humble origins as the Storrs Agricultural School
in 1881, it grew in size and mission over the next six decades and
eventually was designated as the state's public university in 1939.[1]
Though it has a more modest reputation than Yale, UConn has
served many of the state's citizens and has gained an important
position in Connecticut's higher education landscape. It has
125,000 alumni, and claims to have had "direct contact" with over
a million state residents through its various programs, athletic
competitions, extension services and other community-oriented
activities. It has also been successful in attracting substantial research funding and has enhanced its national reputation.[2]

Despite its successes and the fact that it is a public institution
in a state that is often cited as one of the wealthiest in the nation,
at times the University of Connecticut has had difficulty muster-
ing support in the state capital. Though not far from Hartford, it
sometimes has seemed very far removed from the seat of power
politically. In the 1970s, when the state economy was precarious,

it was often difficult for the university to forge effective political alliances. In that era, there was little to suggest that the university was regarded as a particularly important priority by political elites. Instead, other problems and political battles captured the spotlight, and the university seemed to rank low on the state agenda. As a consequence, the reputation of the university suffered.

This troubled situation was not difficult to discern. The *New York Times* described the condition of public higher education in Connecticut this way:

> Connecticut has a major problem with quality. Unlike New York, which has a number of high-quality universities, Connecticut has none. A student interested in an academically demanding education must either make it into a selective independent college such as Yale or Wesleyan, or go out of state. Only some of the community colleges are highly regarded. . . . There is a certain irony because the state ranks second in the country (after Alaska) in per capita income. . . . [However,] wealth does not translate into funds for the University of Connecticut.[3]

Faculty unionization at the University of Connecticut was deeply connected to the vicissitudes of the state's political and economic climates. Other controversies on campus played a part, of course, but as a milieu that was hospitable to faculty unionism began to develop, it was increasingly evident that many campus tensions had external origins.

When sympathy for the idea of unionization emerged among members of the faculty in the early 1970s, there was one significant obstacle: at that time Connecticut state law did not permit state employees to engage in collective bargaining. Therefore, as circumstances led some faculty members to consider the unionization route as an attractive one, it remained a moot point due to the lack of enabling legislation. In addition to addressing other faculty issues, then, union-minded faculty leaders would find it necessary to join the political fight to win public-sector bargaining rights. That would not be an easy task.

ECONOMIC AND POLITICAL CONTEXTS

By some measures, Connecticut was, indeed, a wealthy state in the 1970s. Its per capita income for 1969 of $4,537 was cited as the highest in the nation. At the same time, however, per capita debt was the fourth highest in the United States.[4] As the economic picture for the state darkened, there were signs that state spending could be a problem in the future.

Republican gubernatorial candidate Thomas J. Meskill won a close race for the governor's office in the fall of 1970. His administration inherited what he later called "horrendous financial problems," including a deficit of over $260 million.[5] The seriousness of the fiscal situation was perhaps the state's most pressing problem, and it was regularly a leading topic in the news media.

In the months following his inauguration, the new governor was often successful in setting the agenda for state government. To observers, it seemed that the rival Democratic Party in the state was falling into an increasing state of disarray. The state economic crisis remained a continuing topic of debate at the capitol. It was a topic on which the governor and the General Assembly often disagreed, and the governor vetoed legislation with frequency.

Yet, Governor Meskill was determined to address the economic situation. He searched for new sources of funding and instituted cost-saving measures. In the process, he made cuts in state jobs. Between the beginning of January 1971 and September of 1972, about 1,800 full-time positions were eliminated in state government.[6] By July of 1971, significant budget cuts were announced in an effort to save $120 million.[7] It was apparent the funding that would be made available to state programs and institutions was under close scrutiny.

Governor Meskill and some in the university community had a strained relationship almost from the start of his administration. Fiscal problems were a large part of this story, but not the only part. Some faculty members disapproved of the governor's involvement with the boards of trustees of the university and the other public institutions of higher education. They believed that the governor was inappropriately intruding into university affairs, and they feared the introduction of new political pressures in board decisions.

When, in 1971, Governor Meskill stated that the University of Connecticut's board of trustees was not sufficiently accountable to the taxpayers, some members of the UConn faculty interpreted this as a troubling sign. Meskill's statement elicited a particularly unhappy response from the UConn chapter of the AAUP (UConn-

AAUP), which criticized the governor for allegedly failing to respect the "autonomy and integrity" of Connecticut public institutions of higher education. Whatever his intent, the governor's comments had heightened the impression among some members of the faculty that university matters were increasingly subject to outside meddling.[8] Given the governor's resolve to make improvements in the state's fiscal situation and the University of Connecticut's tenuous claims to the attentions of lawmakers, university officials had some difficulties obtaining resources from the state. In general, these were challenging times for university officials. Facing increasing strains between himself and the governor's administration, in the autumn of 1971 the president of the university, Homer Babbidge, announced that he would leave his position the following year. Many members of the faculty viewed this development with concern. Indeed, the university chapter of the Federation of University Teachers (F.U.T.), an affiliate of the AFL-CIO, subsequently suggested that Babbidge's exit was the result of a "vendetta."[9]

A few months after his announcement, Babbidge's affiliation with the Democratic Party was confirmed in the *Hartford Courant*, which seemed to imply that partisan politics had played some role. Saddled with lame-duck status, the revelation of Babbidge's political leanings (and rumors of a possible gubernatorial bid) cannot have helped matters in his dealings with the Meskill administration.[10]

In the following year, Governor Meskill seemed to be promoting his own candidate for the presidential post, and some interpreted this as yet another attempted intrusion into university matters. Members of the UConn-AAUP and the F.U.T. were already disturbed by unfolding developments at the university. They were especially wary of continued interventions from the governor. In a *Special Newsletter*, the F.U.T. made these statements:

[The governor] should not mess around in the selection of a president of the University of Connecticut. . . . He has a Board of Trustees that he is slowly stacking with run-of-the-mill members. . . . The vendetta which Mr. Meskill launched to get Dr. Babbidge out, succeeded. . . . Help! friends of the University, help![11]

The dramatic nature of this rhetoric notwithstanding, the university faced daunting circumstances on several fronts. In the fall of 1972, the budget request for the coming academic year was reduced because of decreases in enrollment. In addition, the economic travails of the state had a negative impact on university finances, including salaries, while inflation was becoming a national problem.

The salary issue emerged as a major source of tension within the faculty. In 1973, no incremental salary increase was given to UConn faculty. The fact that such increases had been awarded to other state employees exacerbated the already poor reception that this development received from the faculty.[12] Increasingly, UConn faculty members came to believe that they were not faring as well as other state workers, and frustration with this situation was growing.

DEVELOPMENTS IN STATE LABOR RELATIONS

During this period, members of the university faculty, especially those affiliated with the F.U.T. and the UConn-AAUP chapter, were well aware that the unionization movement was gaining ground in higher education. Whatever thoughts they may have had about this course of action as a solution to UConn's ongoing problems remained purely speculative, however, since Connecticut still lacked an enabling statute that would permit the faculty to engage in collective bargaining.

It was not that the issue had failed to attract attention in the legislature. In the early 1970s, the matter of collective bargaining rights for Connecticut state employees was raised several times. The Connecticut General Assembly had considered such legislation in 1970 and again the following year. Both attempts were unsuccessful. Another attempt in 1972 was approved by the Assembly, but was then vetoed by Governor Meskill. With the General Assembly lacking the votes to override the governor's veto, the matter was temporarily put to rest.[13]

By that time, however, the idea seemed to have gained some momentum. Apparently sensing that the issue would continue to resurface, the governor created the Commission on Public Employment Relations in May of 1972. The commission was charged with developing the framework that could shape future legislative initiatives concerning collective negotiations for state employees.[14] Although this development did move the issue along on the state agenda, approval remained several years away.

Glenn W. Ferguson had become the president of the university in the fall of 1973. He came from a three-year tenure as president of Clark University in Worcester, Massachusetts, after having served as the U.S. ambassador to Kenya for several years. During the first two years of his administration, the vacillating circumstances in the state political arena and the insecurities and unrest among the faculty wrought by continued financial pressures led to faculty perceptions that fundamental alterations in working conditions would be forthcoming.

Tenure was one key element of faculty life that seemed to be in jeopardy, heightening tensions within the faculty. Disputes centered on the appropriate roles of the faculty, the administration, and the board in making determinations on tenure. Tenure controversies seemed to be escalating the level of mistrust between faculty and administration.[15] To the UConn-AAUP, in particular, it appeared that there were more cases of tenure denial than in the past. The group also felt that the reasons for these denials were unclear and obscure.[16]

In the summer of 1974, anxiety about this issue escalated among the faculty. This came about when it was reported that President Ferguson had recently remarked that "One issue to be realistically evaluated this year will be the question of alternatives to tenure."[17] Some of the faculty feared the possibility that long-term contracts would be instituted in its place.[18] As would be expected, this was seen as a challenge to what many faculty members viewed as a central tenet in the academic profession. It was not a welcome development by either the UConn-AAUP or the F.U.T.

Feeling threatened and frustrated, the faculty groups became increasingly vocal about their desires for the legal right to bargain collectively. In 1974, the F.U.T. declared:

This is the year to press for collective bargaining. The time is right; the need is urgent. As the university has grown it has become increasingly difficult for the faculty and student voices to be heard.[19]

CHANGE IN STATE POLITICS

By 1974, pressure to enact such legislation was mounting. The state's Office of Legislative Research reported that many states permitted collective bargaining for public employees, giving the impression that Connecticut was slightly behind other states in this area.[20] All the surrounding states had already adopted such measures. Moreover, Congress was considering national legislation greatly extending the rights of collective bargaining among public employees throughout the country.[21]

In March of 1974, Governor Meskill announced that he would not seek re-election. Meskill had made difficult choices and battled with the Democrats in the General Assembly; on balance, however, Connecticut's fiscal situation seemed better, if only temporarily. The prospect of his departure gave renewed hope to public-employee groups pressing for movement on the collective bargaining issue.

In state elections in November 1974, Democratic gubernatorial candidate Ella Grasso easily defeated her Republican opponent, Robert H. Steele. This development, combined with large Democratic majorities in the two chambers of the General Assembly, signaled new attitudes toward many facets of state government. Connecticut still faced fiscal problems, however, and the uncertain economic outlook continued to be a pressing concern.

Early in 1975, with the new Democratic governor sworn into office, legislation was again proposed that would enable state employees to engage in collective bargaining. Prospects for its approval looked brighter than at any time in recent memory. The proposed measure pleased the pro-union groups at the university. Under provisions of the proposal, the faculties of various institutions of higher education would be divided into separate bargaining units. Any unit adopting collective bargaining would then negotiate with its own board of trustees.[22]

Over the next weeks, the bill continued to wend its way through the legislature. In March, the Committee on Public Personnel and Military Affairs conducted hearings on this issue.[23] By that time, an alternative mechanism had been proposed, and there were two bills under consideration. The first would have consolidated all state employees under one umbrella, while a second bill stipulated that local units would be established and would conduct their own negotiations. Faculty groups such as the UConn-AAUP greatly favored the second approach. In addition, they especially wanted legislation that would grant "free choice, by secret ballot, of the exclusive bargaining agent for any designated bargaining unit."[24] The fate of the legislation remained undecided into the summer.

At the Storrs campus, late in the spring of 1975 members of the UConn-AAUP were optimistic and prepared for the day when unionization would be possible.[25] News of the latest version of the state budget added urgency to these efforts. It appeared that the budget would not contain either cost-of-living adjustments or salary increases. With this disappointing turn of events as a backdrop, members of the UConn-AAUP formally made their intentions known to seek the right to be the exclusive bargaining agent for the faculty as soon as enabling legislation was signed into law.[26] The F.U.T. had already made known its intentions to organize the faculty.

That summer, during the final hours of the 1975 session of the General Assembly, collective bargaining rights were approved for state workers along strict party lines. Republican members of the Assembly had vigorously opposed the measure, but their numbers were too few to prevent passage of the legislation.[27] Governor Grasso, who had supported the initiative, subsequently signed the bill into law. It would become effective in October of that year.

THE CAMPAIGN BEGINS

With bargaining rights secured, the drive to gather the required signatures to petition for an election began in earnest. Faculty unrest on the UConn campus at Storrs had increased over the years that collective bargaining had been an issue at the state level. Consequently, among many members of the faculty a strong inclination toward unionization had already crystallized by the time the law went into effect. There would be no protracted hand wringing about whether to push for a union; it was a question of which group, the UConn-AAUP or the F.U.T., would gather the required number of signed cards first. Many thought that the

F.U.T. had the edge, but it seemed likely that both would reach the ballot.

Even before collective bargaining had been approved by the state, competition between the UConn chapter of the F.U.T. and the UConn-AAUP had emerged. When enabling legislation was finally signed into law, the competition between the two potential bargaining agents increased. There was some discussion about a possible merger of the two campus groups, but there was insufficient agreement for that idea to go forward. As explained by the UConn-AAUP, the rejection of a merger was a matter rooted in "important philosophical differences" between the two organizations.[28]

Instead, the two groups vied for favor among the faculty. Various approaches were used in these efforts. In promoting itself over the F.U.T., for example, the UConn-AAUP noted that AAUP affiliates at the University of Rhode Island and Rutgers had recently bargained for substantial salary increases (12 percent and 18 percent, respectively). The group said that if it were selected as the bargaining agent, the UConn-AAUP would similarly aim to establish "minimum salary scales for each rank which will bring the University up to the level of comparable institutions."[29] The F.U.T., of course, disagreed with the view that an AAUP group would have the best chance of successfully negotiating for the faculty and made counterarguments to that effect.[30]

One prime area of disagreement was in each group's basic approach to collective bargaining. According to the UConn-AAUP, the rival F.U.T. employed an approach that was too "industrial." Underscoring, this view was the F.U.T.'s connection to its parent organization, the American Federation of Teachers, an AFL-CIO affiliate That contrasted with the UConn-AAUP group's perception that the AAUP approach was "more professional."[31]

On the other hand, the UConn-AAUP was sometimes placed on the defensive, countering the suggestion that it would not be strong enough to serve as an effective advocate in collective bargaining. In response to such arguments, the group issued a statement declaring that "The people who think that the AAUP is a 'pussyfooting' organization fail to recognize that it is the only national organization vigorously supporting academic freedom and tenure."[32]

As the campaign progressed, the two groups continued to press for the advantage with the faculty. Still, the level of acrimony between the competing groups remained somewhat constrained by the recognition of their mutual goal.

THE ADMINISTRATION REACTS

Details of the Act Concerning Collective Bargaining for State Employees was relayed to deans, directors and department heads shortly after the beginning of the fall semester. They learned that the act granted self-organization rights to employees, as well as the right to bargain in an environment free from interference, restraint, or coercion.[33] The act contained typical features in establishing a mechanism for the establishment of collective bargaining. To petition for an election, a group was required to gather signed cards from at least 30 percent of the members in the proposed bargaining unit. An additional group, if there were one, would then need to obtain cards from only another 10 percent of the members to appear on the ballot. In the election itself (which also would automatically contain a ballot slot for the "no bargaining agent" alternative), a choice would need to gain more than 50 percent of the votes to decide the matter. If no choice met that threshold, a runoff election was mandated.[34]

The university sought advice about how it should proceed. Some sources suggested that university should retain independent legal counsel, rather than relying on the state for that purpose. Experts had recommended that this would be especially helpful in dealing with the issue of who would and would not be included in the bargaining unit.

This advice, however, directly contradicted the wishes of the state administration. In a meeting in September 1975, Jay Tepper, the state commissioner of finance and control, informed representatives from the public institutions of higher education that Governor Grasso wanted to centralize collective bargaining negotiations with all of the public colleges and universities. The intention was to do this through the Commission on Higher Education. This idea generated a cool response from the various boards of trustees, who viewed the respective boards as independent entities.[35]

A week later, Tepper called UConn leaders to reiterate the state administration's position that all collective negotiations with state employees should be coordinated through a single legal firm that it had selected. Meanwhile, the UConn Board of Trustees obtained approval from the state attorney general's office to use its own counsel. That office held the view that the governor did not have the authority to demand otherwise.[36]

As the reality of a campaign to organize the University of Connecticut faculty at Storrs set in, the administration began to weigh possible responses to it. One senior administrator journeyed to Boston to meet with legal counsel about the anticipated collective bargaining campaign. In the course of the meeting, the counsel and UConn administrator apparently discussed several hypothetical responses to a union-organizing campaign.[37]

The possibilities that were raised in the discussion showed that the administration was weighing all its options. The university could take one of three stances regarding a union: in favor, neutral, or opposed. Ways to legally discourage unionization were pondered as one possibility. In one such scenario the university would initially take a neutral public stance about unionization. Later in the campaign, this would allow the administration to announce that it had thoroughly deliberated on the matter and only at that point had determined that collective bargaining would be a detrimental change.[38] This idea, which would have required the university to adopt a rather Machiavellian posture if it had already decided that it did not want a union, was apparently not pursued beyond a hypothetical scenario. In any case, it is difficult to imagine such a plan being very effective, particularly since many pro-union faculty members were already quite skeptical of the board and administration. It seems unlikely that they would have looked to the administration for guidance about their decision.

Another possible strategy that was raised would have involved encouraging the development of an anti-union group of faculty members.[39] This strategy would have provided a way for faculty opposition to collective bargaining to be heard from within the faculty's own ranks, rather than from the administration. Official administrative sponsorship of such a group would not be possible, of course, and in any case would undercut such a group's credibility with other faculty members. Even if such a group emerged spontaneously from faculty ranks, too much support emanating from the administration would give the impression that the group was merely acting as a mouthpiece for an anti-union administration.

Although some, perhaps most, members of the administration preferred not to see a faculty union at UConn, experience elsewhere showed that this was a strong possibility. Members of the administration could at least take comfort in the fact that some members of the faculty volunteered to make the case against a union. It was faculty members who represented the "no agent" position at events such as a forum sponsored by the Labor Education Center. Still, the administration seemed to have realized that it would not be able to direct the outcome of events. The victory in gaining bargaining rights from the state had invigorated the pro-union forces in the faculty, and they would be difficult to defeat.

By late in the fall semester, it was clear that an election would be forthcoming. At the December meeting of the board of trustees, it was reported that the UConn-AAUP would imminently file its petition with the state board of labor relations.[40] Within the administration, the attitude toward the increasing likelihood of a faculty union ranged from antipathy to resignation. One high-level administrator attended meetings of a regional group called the Academy for Academic Personnel Administration and heard stories about the situation at other campuses. Ostensibly this group provided a venue for administrators from various institutions to share information, but it also functioned as a support group for disillusioned administrators grappling with faculty unionization issues.[41]

Indeed, the documents recording the administration's work on the collective bargaining issue reveal the same disillusionment at Storrs. Though administrators had thoroughly researched the experiences of other universities regarding faculty unionization, the realization that collective bargaining seemed to be at hand still seems to have been a bitter pill for some members of the administration to swallow. Undoubtedly, the increasing rhetoric arising from the competition between the F.U.T. and UConn-AAUP did not help the situation.

CONTROVERSY ABOUT UNIT DETERMINATION

Determining who would be eligible for membership in the potential bargaining unit was one major source of controversy within the administration. The UConn-AAUP and the F.U.T. initially adopted a similar line, favoring a single bargaining unit that would include faculty members, department heads, and librarians. In addition to objecting to inclusion of department heads, however, the administration took exception to the idea of including librarians in a unit composed primarily of teaching faculty. The UConn-AAUP position was that the university library was suffering and was "badly understaffed," and they wanted librarians in the unit. They held the view that "the Administration is badly mistaken in refusing to recognize librarians as part of the faculty."[42]

When it appeared that the disagreement about the composition of the bargaining unit would result in a postponement of the election, some compromise was reached between the administration and the faculty groups. At first, both the F.U.T. and the UConn-AAUP reluctantly agreed to exclude librarians from the proposed unit. They hoped for an election in April and did not want to see it delayed. Then, however, the F.U.T. pulled out of that agreement and reiterated its position that librarians should be included.[43] Although the UConn-AAUP claimed that the change in position was merely an "election strategy" on the part of the F.U.T.,[44] the dispute threatened to derail the election process. In fact, both faculty groups seem to have been involved in strategic maneuvering on the issue, since the UConn-AAUP continued to claim that the librarians belonged in the unit. The disagreement, therefore, was not rooted in differing policy positions, but rather in whether the fight over the librarians' status was worth the potential cost that a delayed election might have.

The impasse about the librarians' status resulted in some public bickering about what group was responsible for the apparent setback in the collective bargaining campaign. Seeking to "salvage an early election,"[45] the UConn-AAUP petitioned the State Labor Relations Board to abide by the original election dates under a provision in state law. Under the UConn-AAUP proposal, the contested issue would be addressed by impounding librarians' ballots until the matter had been resolved.[46] The situation moved toward resolution with an agreement about election dates that was reached among the parties.[47] As suggested in the UConn-AAUP's petition, the librarian issue was separated from the election date issue, and a hearing on that issue was set for later in the month.[48] (Resolution of the librarians' status would not come until after the election.)

CAMPAIGN ISSUES

Members of the faculty had raised many issues in the preceding years. These and newer matters were now brought up as the campaign to build support for a faculty union became more intense. The salary issue remained at the forefront. Faculty salaries continued to languish, although other state employees had fared somewhat better. One such beneficiary of state largesse was the commissioner of higher education, who was awarded a 10 percent salary increase in October of 1975.[49]

Voicing a keen sense of frustration, the UConn-AAUP addressed the issue of faculty salaries:

In the last five years the average purchasing power of all Americans increased 3 per cent in constant dollars; in academe it has *decreased* [italics in original] 8 per cent; at UConn it has *decreased 18 per cent* [sic].

What does the average UConn faculty member need just to catch up?

To catch up with other academic institutions—10%

To catch up with our own 1970–1971 buying power—18%

To catch up with the average American—21%[50]

Meanwhile, the state's fiscal situation had become worse, further dampening hopes that university funding and faculty salaries would rise under the existing arrangements. The plight of the state economy was not difficult to see. In May of 1975, the state's bond rating dropped. The inflation rate was estimated at 12 percent.[51] In November, Governor Grasso called a special session of the General Assembly in response to the state deficit, which had surpassed $80 million. In the following month, unemployment reached a record-high level. Such circumstances both threatened

the general economic outlook for the university and heightened faculty concerns about job security.
As 1975 drew to a close, the UConn-AAUP reported on the situation with some urgency. The group argued:

The "new" fiscal crisis in the state's finances and the renewed awareness of how vulnerable all state employees are to shifting state administrations and policies testify to the urgent need to have *legally binding contracts* [sic] which can only be gained under collective bargaining.[52]

Proposals to ease the state's financial woes did little to ease faculty unrest. In one response, the presidents of the UConn-AAUP, F.U.T., along with the head of the UConn Professional Employees Association, signed a joint statement condemning the "inequitable new patchwork proposals" that the governor had proposed to address the state's fiscal problems. In a joint statement they wrote:

State employees seem to be the chosen scapegoats for some politicians. Employees lost purchasing power; yet their work did not decrease. In effect, they were involuntarily subsidizing the state's general fund. Now many are being asked to work extra hours without any pay raise at all.[53]

In January of 1976, members of the UConn-AAUP, the F.U.T., and the Professional Employees Association met with the chair of the Appropriations Committee and lobbied for increased university funding. This action, which bypassed the university administration and board altogether, showed that faculty groups were willing to take their case directly to Hartford. Increasingly, the faculty's perception was that the administration and the board could not be effective advocates on their behalf. Moreover, the connections between faculty unionization efforts and organized labor were coming to the fore. The F.U.T. had recently quoted a letter it received from John Driscoll, president of the Connecticut State Labor Council, stating that "the State AFL-CIO Labor Council is prepared to provide every assistance that it possibly can" in the UConn organizing effort.[54]

Other issues also contributed to faculty dissatisfaction. A change in parking regulations on campus, for example, had been greeted negatively by faculty members, some of whom regarded the new procedures as further evidence that the faculty was not well respected by the administration and had little influence over even simple matters. Small changes such as this, which may have been benign in intent, nonetheless came to exemplify the need for unionization. They presented union-minded faculty with yet another case to use as a rallying cry for collective bargaining. The possibility that teaching loads might change in the future presented a somewhat more urgent issue. The F.U.T. believed that this was a genuine possibility. The group's November 1975 newsletter stated:

In Rhode Island the University was the last of the state's institutions of higher education to enter the field of collective bargaining. Since the legislature had earlier experience in dealing with higher education institutions (state and community colleges) with significantly higher teaching loads than the University, it became increasingly difficult for the University to explain the research component of a university scholar's workload. "Why," some legislators asked, "shouldn't the university faculty also teach 12 or 15 hours a week?"[55]

In the background were most of the other concerns that had been expressed throughout the decade, including tenure. During a period that had seen change and uncertainty, the collective power of a union remained an appealing idea to many members of the faculty.

THE ELECTION

The election was held in early April 1976, and the results were conclusive. Of 1,038 ballots cast, the UConn-AAUP received 549 votes (53% of those voting), the Federation of University Teachers group received 296 votes (just over 28%) and the "no agent" alternative polled only 174 votes (just over 16%). (There were also 19 challenged ballots and an additional 89 ballots cast by librarians, whose membership in the proposed unit was still the subject of dispute.)[56]

In June, the State Board of Labor Relations certified the vote and UConn-AAUP's status as the faculty's bargaining agent. It also ruled against inclusion of librarians in the faculty unit; the librarians were subsequently included in a unit of nonteaching professionals at the university that was in the process of formation.[57]

Internal controversies about matters ranging from tenure to parking regulations had played a role in unionism among the faculty, but it was conditions in the state political and economic environments that fueled its rise on campus. The story also was entwined with the emergence of state-employee bargaining rights in the state. Although there was limited public discourse about the unionization of the UConn faculty per se, the broader issues in which it was embedded were frequently covered by the news media. In this indirect fashion, public discourse played an important role in shaping the milieu that fostered unionism among the faculty.

NOTES

1. Along the way to university status, the Storrs Agricultural School underwent several name changes. It became the Storrs Agricultural College in 1893, was renamed the Connecticut Agricultural College in 1899, and became Connecticut State College in 1933.

2. These are among the statements made in *The University of Connecticut Graduate Catalog, 1996/97.* The research funding that was noted also includes that of the University of Connecticut Health Center campus, which is not located on the main campus at Storrs.

3. Quoted in Federation of University Teachers, Newsletter, 21 March 1977. (Located in the University Archives, University of Connecticut, Storrs, hereafter referred to as UCA.)

4. These figures, originally published in the *Hartford Courant*, are cited in Charles L. Towne, *Hartford Courant Index*, (bound photocopy in the collection of the Babbidge Library, University of Connecticut, Storrs),v. 23 n.p.

5. See *The Trinity Reporter*, Winter 1998.

6. "Meskill claims 1,801 fulltime [*sic*] jobs cut," *Hartford Courant*, 13 September 1972.

7. "State orders 11½% cutback," *Hartford Courant*, 11 July 1971.

8. "Professor critical of governor," *Hartford Courant*, 20 May 1971.

9. Federation of University Teachers, *Special Newsletter*, August 1972, UCA.

10. Later, in 1973, the differences between the two men were highlighted when Babbidge revealed that he was interested in becoming the Democratic candidate in the next gubernatorial race.

11. Federation of University Teachers, Memorandum [August ca.] 1972, UCA.

12. AAUP, University of Connecticut Chapter, *Summary of AAUP Report,* April 1973, UCA.

13. Office of Legislative Research, Legislative Commissioner's Office, Connecticut General Assembly, "Collective Bargaining for State Employees: Issues and Laws," Interim Report No. 3, 1974, 68. UCA.

14. Ibid., 74.

15. See A.T. DiBenedetto, Letter to Gordon Tasker, 17 July 1974, UCA.

16. See A.T. DiBenedetto, Letter to Gordon Tasker, 26 August 1974, UCA.

17. *AAUP Vanguard: Connecticut Conference of the American Association of University Professors,* September 1974, 2, UCA.

18. Ibid.

19. Federation of University Teachers, Memorandum, n.d., 1974, UCA.

20. Office of Legislative Research, Legislative Commissioner's Office, Connecticut General Assembly, "Collective Bargaining for State Employees: Issues and Laws," Interim Report No. 3, 1974, 90, UCA.

21. Ibid., 79

22. See State of Connecticut, General Assembly, Legislative Commissioner's Office, No. 8424, January Session, 1975, UCA.

23. See Connecticut Chapter, AAUP, Newsletter, April 1975.

24. Ibid.

25. The faculty of the medical campus showed little interest in unionizing and is not included in this discussion.

26. See Connecticut Chapter, AAUP, Newsletter, May 1975.

27. Irene Driscoll, "Pay Raises Clear as Assembly Adjourns," *Hartford Courant,* 5 June 1975.

28. UConn-AAUP , Newsletter, 28 October 1975, UCA.

29. See UConn-AAUP, Newsletter, 26 September 1975, UCA.

30. Federation of University Teachers, Newsletter (ca. May 1975), UCA.

31. Ibid.

32. See UConn-AAUP, Newsletter, September 1975, UCA.

33. See Bertram W. Wilson, Memorandum to Deans, Directors, and Department Heads, 24 September 1975, UCA.

34. This was outlined to UConn faculty in UConn-AAUP, Newsletter, September 1975, UCA.

35. John G. Hill, Memorandum to G. Ferguson, 1 October 1975, UCA.

36. John G. Hill, Memorandum to G. Ferguson, 9 October 1975, UCA.

37. This meeting was recounted in detail in a memorandum, now in the university archives. See J. Geetter, Memorandum to K. Wilson, 8 September 1975, UCA.

38. Ibid.

39. Ibid.

40. Board of Trustees, University of Connecticut, Memorandum, 12 December 1975, UCA.

41. See Geetter.

42. UConn-AAUP Newsletter, 18 February 1976.

43. Ibid.

44. UConn-AAUP Newsletter, 18 February 1976, UCA

45. UConn-AAUP Newsletter, 23 February 1976, UCA

46. UConn Chapter AAUP Newsletter, 2 March 1976, UCA

47. UConn Chapter AAUP Newsletter, 10 March 1976, UCA

48. Ibid.

49. "Louis Rabineau, Higher Education Commissioner Gets 4K raise," *Hartford Courant,* 22 October 1975.

50. UConn-AAUP Newsletter, 28 October 1975, UCA.

51. See Driscoll.

52. UConn-AAUP Newsletter, 5 December 1975, UCA

53. UConn-AAUP Newsletter, 5 December 1975, UCA.

54. Quoted in Federation of University Teachers, Newsletter, 8 December 1975.

55. Federation of University Teachers, Newsletter, 10 November 1975, UCA.

56. UConn-AAUP, Newsletter, 12 April 1976, UCA.

57. UConn-AAUP, Newsletter, 10 June 1976, UCA.

CHAPTER 7

Epilogue

The rise of faculty unionism among college and university faculties has been a multifaceted phenomenon, of which the stories of the University of Rhode Island, the University of Massachusetts and the University of Connecticut represent only a part. Each campus that wrestles with the question of a faculty union faces some particular characteristics that are unique to that time and setting. Indeed, one lesson that can be gleaned from the events recounted in the preceding chapters is that it would be a mistake to oversimplify the causes and motivations that drive the unionization process. Especially in the public sector, the number of actors and observers who have a bearing on the outcome of a union organizing drive may be large, and the interplay among them difficult to predict.

The transformation of the flagship public universities of southern New England into faculty union environments was rooted in many circumstances inherent in the political and economic climate of the region in the 1970s. The coalescing of several streams of events created circumstances that made collective bargaining, if not attractive outright, then, at least, preferable to the status quo.

Talk of the creation of faculty unions sometimes emerges from local antagonisms between faculty, on the one hand, and administrations (and boards of trustees), on the other. Those conflicts may be relatively small scale—such as the threatened loss of office phones or changes in parking regulations—or they may strike closer to the central features of faculty life, such as a proposed change in tenure policies or the perception of a diminished faculty role in campus decision making.

A perceived threat to established tenure policies is one of the most potent of these issues. In many employment sectors, employees may change employers several, or sometimes many, times. Many professionals move from one corporate setting to another in order to advance their careers. It is commonly believed that professionals can obtain greater rewards—in terms of financial compensation and prestige—by moving from one organization to another while climbing the career ladder. This pattern is not unusual among college and university administrators, but it is relatively rare among university professors. For university faculty members careers are often played out in only one or two organizations. Therefore, tenure, which provides some measure of assurance about the continuation of the employment relationship along lines that are more or less understood in advance, becomes a valued aspect of academic life.

When uncertainty over matters such as these are combined with contentious salary issues, collective bargaining becomes more appealing. In all three of the southern New England states, this was a compelling reason for the faculties to seriously consider collective bargaining. Faculty unionism there was a response to deteriorating economic circumstances, or to a perception that faculty members would be subject to economic cutbacks. Administrations and boards were the source of significant frustrations on bread and butter issues among these faculties. In many respects, however, university authorities held limited control over the overall fiscal situations of their respective institutions. Because university budgets were tied to state budgets and economic conditions, university officials' room for maneuvering was severely constrained.

To a considerable degree, then, the drive to unionize these faculties was rooted in concerns about actual or envisioned changes in working conditions and compensation. Certainly, there would have been little motivation to adopt collective bargaining if it were not for these. Beyond the substance of the changes, however, was the symbolic value associated with them. Symbolically, situations emerging on campus suggested that faculty power was eroding. Although existing mechanisms for power sharing, such as faculty senates, had evolved to provide the faculties with a role in university decision making, these now seemed increasingly ineffective. The general unrest of the period had already strained these organizations, and confidence that they could satisfactorily address faculty concerns had waned, at least in the eyes of some faculty members.

Unionization at these campuses occurred during a period when the density of such developments was great. The contagion-like spread of unionism as an idea that could be relevant to academic communities was an important factor in the rise of unionism on these campuses. As the traditional ways of doing things seemed to yield increasingly disappointing results, the existence of a ready-made and tested model made the unionization choice a shorter step for these faculties than would otherwise have been the case. Not only had the apparent utility of the union model been demonstrated; just as important, as the practice continued to spread across the various strata of higher education, the legitimacy of faculty unions became increasingly enhanced. Though opponents of faculty unionization saw the situation differently, the faculties could easily point to colleagues at other institutions to reassure themselves that they were exploring a legitimate course of action. Faculty unionism, in this view, can therefore be seen as much more than the result of purely local situations.

Although faculty influence on these and other campuses had increased over time, the crises of the era heightened awareness of the asymmetrical division of power on these campuses. The coming of unionism also represented a strong challenge to the power of administrations and governing boards.

Enter the larger world of state employee relations. Traditionally, university faculties and workers in other state enterprises believed they had little in common. However, strains in state fiscal conditions heightened the awareness that faculty economic circumstances were closely associated with the overall economic picture in the state. As state resources became scarcer, faculty members began to realize that the fate of faculty salaries was entangled in the larger picture of state public payrolls. Even though the public universities had some degree of autonomy, the financial dependence on state legislatures was a limiting factor. As other state workers turned to collective bargaining to bolster their clout in this situation, it increased pressure on faculties to do the same.

In addition, from the faculty perspective the implication was that those segments of the public labor force that unionized would reap the bulk of the benefits for themselves. Non-unionized employees risked being left by the wayside. Therefore, the rise of faculty unionism in such cases can be interpreted as a defensive measure for increasing the effectiveness of group advocacy in a crowded public employee environment, in which other groups have union representation.

In these circumstances, the resources that the national faculty organizations could offer became another force that helped to propel the drive toward unionization.

As William A. Gamson has noted, a crisis "can aid those challengers who have established their presence before the crisis occurs." Along these lines, the existence of campus chapters of the national associations prior to the economic decline and faculty strife at the time of rising faculty unionism was important.[1] The affiliates of the national associations provided the faculties with important access to knowledge, organizing skill, personnel, and funding. University administrations and governing boards were unaccustomed to dealing with this sort of external influence. Sometimes, their responses were oddly unsophisticated and seemed to be based on the dubious assumption that faculties looked to them for advice. The apparent belief held by some (though not all) administrative leaders, that they could explain to faculties why a union would be a poor choice, was probably a naive one from the start. (Not even Henry Ford had been able to stave off unionization indefinitely.)

In general, the presence of national associations and the power they represented, combined with the understanding that the universities were tied to the states' economic situations, were powerful incentives to adopt the collective bargaining mechanisms.

The attention of the news media was another element in the process of faculty unionization on these campuses. In general, the press closely linked the public universities to state government. The degree to which the news media directed attention to events surrounding unionization was varied among these cases, but in general the news media did help to create the milieu in which the unionization events played out. In the case of Rhode Island, for example, coverage of the faculty salary issue was at times linked to the overall stature and quality of the University of Rhode Island. The character of the news coverage helped to define for its audience the relative importance of faculty unionization as an issue and to identify the salient issues in faculty unionism in a context of the respective state's political realm.[2]

On a more conceptual level, faculty unionism was a response to the lessening of a shared vision of academic life between faculties, on the one hand, and governing and administrative authorities, on the other. Even by the 1970s, some of the central ideas about academic life were deeply contested, as the questions about tenure policies revealed. There is a built-in tension between the governing boards, which hold formal authority, and faculties, which provide the core services of teaching and scholarship. In a general sense, a bifurcation of world views between the two groups seems evident. Boards often show a tendency to view the academic world from a business perspective, while academics view it from their professional perspectives. Though this oversimplifies the situation, one can reasonably conclude that, on many matters, governing boards and faculties have fundamental differences when it comes to values. When differences in power between the two groups are added to this picture, a complicated relationship emerges.

Although the decision about whether to unionize is made collectively by the faculty, not all members of a faculty will agree with the outcome. Individuals, as well as different collectivities, may hold contrasting world views and judgments about the efficacy and appropriateness of unionization. Faculties are no exception. Where collective bargaining is permitted, however, the majority decides for the entirety. When the vote is a close one, there is a potential for lingering resentment. The decision to unionize, or not to unionize, may expose faculty differences and may represent only the beginning of new complexities of campus politics.

In some respects, the unionization of public university faculties raises questions about the place of these institutions as public entities. Though they may have quasi-independent status, their ties to the state are complicating factors. Whatever insulation from state politics is intended (and this is an open question in many cases), the boundaries between public institutions of higher education and the state political realm are very porous. To those who are employed by the institutions, collective bargaining may seem like one protection from the changing political winds.

The decision about whether to adopt collective bargaining is, in one sense, a rational choice. Employees who think that they will be better off with a union than without one might reasonably choose that option. However, a decision to adopt collective bargaining is also a judgment about the state of existing power relationships on campus and about the legitimacy and viability with which those relationships are regarded. In addition, it involves a judgment about what values are most important on campus. These are political and cultural choices, too.

NOTES

1. See William A. Gamson, *The Strategy of Social Protest* (Homewood, IL: The Dorsey Press, 1975), 128.

2. See Bernard Cohen, *The Press and Foreign Policy* (Princeton: Princeton University Press, 1963) and Donald L. Shaw and Maxwell E. McCombs, *The Emergence of American Political Issues: The Agenda-Setting Function of the Press* (Minneapolis: West Publishing Co., 1977).

Works Cited

AAUP Newsletter (University of Massachusetts Chapter). Material in the University Archives, W.E.B. Du Bois Library, University of Massachusetts, Amherst, Mass. Various dates.

Arnold, Gordon. "The Emergence of Faculty Unions at Flagship Public Universities in Southern New England." *Labor Studies Journal*, vol. 22, no. 4 (1998): 62–87.

Arnold, Gordon B., and Ted I. K. Youn. "Evolving Public Discourse of Tenure and Academic Freedom, 1950s–1990s: A Frame Analysis." Paper presented at the Annual Meeting of the Association for the Study of Higher Education, Miami, November 1998.

Aronson, Robert L. "Unionism Among Professional Employees in the Private Sector." *ILR Review*, vol. 38 (1985): 352–64.

Barbrook, Alec T. *God Save the Commonwealth: An Electoral History of Massachusetts*. Amherst: University of Massachusetts Press, 1973.

"Bargaining Activity." *Academe*, vol. 10, no. 1 (1976): 9.

Barrow, Clyde W. *Universities and the Capitalist State: Corporate Liberalism and the Reconstruction of American Higher Education, 1894–1928*. Madison: University of Wisconsin Press, 1990.

Benjamin, Ernst. "Faculty and Management Rights in Higher Education Collective Bargaining: A Faculty Perspective." Paper presented at the 25th Annual Meeting of the Center for the Study of Collective Bargaining in Higher Education and the Professions, New York, 14 April 1997.

Birnbaum, Robert. *Creative Academic Bargaining: Managing Conflict in the Unionized College and University*. New York: Teachers College Press, 1980.

————. *How Colleges Work: The Cybernetics of Academic Organization and Leadership*. San Francisco: Jossey-Bass, 1988.

Bok, Derek C., and John T. Dunlop. *Labor and the American Community*. New York: Simon & Schuster, 1970.

Boston Globe. Various dates.

Boston Herald. Various dates.

Caplow, Theodore, and Reece J. McGee. *The Academic Marketplace*. New York: Science Editions, 1961.

Carr, Robert K., and Daniel K. van Eyck. *Collective Bargaining Comes to the Campus*. Washington, DC: American Council on Education, 1973.

Cary, Harold Whiting. *The University of Massachusetts: A History of One Hundred Years*. Amherst: University of Massachusetts, 1962.

Christian Science Monitor. Various dates.

Chronicle of Higher Education. Various dates.

Clark, Burton R. *The Academic Life: Small Worlds, Different Worlds*. Princeton: The Carnegie Foundation for the Advancement of Teaching, 1987.

Cohen, Bernard. *The Press and Foreign Policy*. Princeton: Princeton University Press, 1963.

Daily Hampshire Gazette. Various dates.

DiMaggio, Paul J., and Walter W. Powell. "The Iron Cage Revisited: Institutional Isomorphism and Collective Rationality in Organizational Fields." *American Sociological Review*, vol. 48 (1983): 147–60.

Duryea, E. D. "Evolution of University Organization" In Marvin W. Peterson (Ed.) *ASHE Reader on Organization and Governance in Higher Education*, 165–82. Needham Heights, MA: Ginn Press, 1988.

Federation of University Teachers Newsletter. Material in the Archives and Special Collections Department, Thomas J. Dodd Research Center, University of Connecticut, Storrs, Conn. Various dates.

Finkin, Matthew W., Robert A. Goldstein, and Woodley B. Osborne. *A Primer on Collective Bargaining for College and University Faculty*. Washington, DC: American Association of University Professors, 1975.

Freeland, Richard M. *Academia's Golden Age: Universities in Massachusetts, 1945–1970*. New York: Oxford University Press, 1992.

Gamson, William A. *The Strategy of Social Protest*. Homewood, IL: Dorsey Press, 1975.

Garbarino, Joseph W., and Bill Aussieker. *Faculty Bargaining: Change and Conflict*. New York: McGraw-Hill, 1975.

Gumport, Patricia J. "Public Universities as Academic Workplaces." *Daedalus*, vol. 126, no. 4 (Fall 1997): 113–36.

Hartford Courant. Various dates.

Jencks, Christopher, and David Riesman. *The Academic Revolution*. New York: Doubleday, 1968.

Johnstone, Ronald L. *The Scope of Faculty Collective Bargaining: An Analysis of Faculty Union Agreements at Four-Year Institutions of Higher Education*. Westport, CT: Greenwood Press, 1981.

Julius, Daniel J. (ed.). *Collective Bargaining in Higher Education: The State of the Art*. Washington, DC: College and University Personnel Association, 1984.

Juravich, Tom, William F. Hartford, and James R. Green. *Commonwealth of Toil: Chapters in the History of Massachusetts Workers and Their Unions*. Amherst: University of Massachusetts Press, 1996.

Keck, Donald J. *The NEA and Academe Through the Years: The Higher Education Roots of the NEA, 1857–Present*. Washington, DC: NEA, 1999.

Kemerer, Frank R., and J. Victor Baldrige. *Unions on Campus*. San Francisco: Jossey-Bass, 1975.

Ladd, Everett Carll, Jr., and Seymour Martin Lipsett. *Professors, Unions, and American Higher Education*. Washington, DC: American Enterprise Institute, 1973.

Laumann, Edward O., and David Knoke. *The Organizational State*. Madison: University of Wisconsin Press, 1987.

Lee, Barbara A., and James P. Begin, "Criteria for Evaluating the Managerial Status of College Faculty: Applications of *Yeshiva University* by the NLRB." *Journal of College and University Law*, vol. 10, no. 4 (Spring 1984): 515–39.

Lewin, David, and Shirley B. Goldenberg. "Public Sector Unionism in the United States and Canada." *Industrial Relations*, vol. 19 (1980): 239–56.

Lindblom, Charles S. *Inquiry and Change: The Troubled Attempt to Understand and Shape Policy*. New Haven: Yale University Press, 1990.

Litt, Edgar. *Political Cultures of Massachusetts*. Cambridge: MIT Press, 1965.

Love, Thomas M., and George T. Sulzner. "Political Implications of Public Employee Bargaining." *Industrial Relations*, vol. 11 (1972): 18–33.

Mass, Michael A., and Anita F. Gottlieb. "Federally Legislated Collective Bargaining for State and Local Government." In *Labor Relations in the Public Sector: Readings and Cases*, 2d ed., ed. Marvin J. Levine, 76–87. Columbus, OH: Publishing Horizons, 1985.

MasSProf Newsletter. Material in the University Archives, W.E.B. Du Bois Library, University of Massachusetts, Amherst, Mass. Various dates.

Miller, Will. "Unionizing at the University of Vermont." *Thought and Action*, vol. 6, no. 1 (Spring 1990): 59–66.

New York Times. Various dates.

Odewahn, Charles A., and Allan D. Spritzer. "Administrators' Attitudes Toward Faculty Unionism." *Industrial Relations*, vol. 15 (1976): 206–15.

Providence Journal. Various dates.

Redenius, Charles. "Public Employees: A Survey of Some Critical Problems on the Frontier of Collective Bargaining." In *Labor Relations in the Public Sector: Readings and Cases*, 2d ed., ed. Marvin J. Levine, 7–22. Columbus, OH: Publishing Horizons, 1985.

Rees, Albert. *The Economics of Trade Unions*. 3rd ed. Chicago: The University of Chicago Press, 1989.

Rhoades, Gary. *Managed Professionals: Unionized Faculty and Restructuring Academic Labor*. Albany: State University of New York Press, 1998.

Riesman, David. "The Academic Procession." In *Constraint and Variety in American Education*, 25–65. Garden City, NY: Doubleday Anchor, 1958.

Riesman, David, and Christopher Jencks. "The Viability of the American College." In *The American College*. ed. Sanford Nevitt. New York: Wiley and Sons, 1962.

Rosenthal, Alan. *Governors and Legislatures: Contending Powers*. Washington, DC: CQ Press, 1990.

Rudolph, Frederick S. *The American College and University: A History*. New York: Alfred A. Knopf, 1962.

Sanford, Nevitt (ed.). *The American College*. New York: Wiley & Sons 1962.

Shaw, Donald L., and Maxwell E. McCombs. *The Emergence of American Political Issues: The Agenda-Setting Function of the Press*. Minneapolis: West Publishing Co., 1977.

Skocpol, Theda, and Kenneth Finegold. "Explaining New Deal Labor Policy." *American Political Science Review*, vol. 84 (1990): 1297–315.

Sloane, Arthur S., and Fred Witney. *Labor Relations*. 6th ed. Englewood Cliffs, NJ: Prentice Hall, 1988.

Summers, Clyde W. "Public Employee Bargaining: A Political Perspective." *Yale Law Journal*, vol. 83 (1974): 1156–200.

UConn-AAUP Newsletter. Material in the Archives and Special Collections Department, Thomas J. Dodd Research Center, University of Connecticut, Storrs, Conn. Various dates.

URIPA Newsletter. Material in the Special Collections and Archives Department, University Library, University of Rhode Island, Kingston, RI. Various dates.

U.S. Department of Labor. Bureau of Labor Statistics. *Handbook of Labor Statistics*. Washington, DC: U.S. Department of Labor, 1989.

Veysey, Laurence R. *The Emergence of the American University*. Chicago: University of Chicago Press, 1965.

Vogel, David. *Fluctuating Fortunes: The Political Power of Business in America*. New York: The Free Press, 1989.

Wellington, Harry H., and Ralph K. Winter, Jr. "The Limits of Collective Bargaining in the Public Sector." In David Lewin, Peter Feuille, and Thomas A. Kochan (Eds.) *Public Sector Labor Relations: Analysis and Readings*. 2nd ed., 24–32. Sun Lakes, AZ: Thomas Horton, 1981.

Winkler, Allan M. "The Faculty Workload Question." *Change*, vol. 24 (July/August 1992): 36–41.

Wood, Floris W. (ed.). *An American Profile: Opinions and Behavior, 1972–1989*. Detroit: Gale Research, 1990.

"Yeshiva-watch: Year Six" *National Center for the Study of Collective Bargaining in Higher Education and the Professions Newsletter*, vol. 13, no. 5 (November/December 1985).

Index

About the Author

GORDON B. ARNOLD is Adjunct Research Associate, Center for Policy Analysis, University of Massachusetts at Dartmouth.